ART
of the
JOB SEARCH

A STEP-BY-STEP GUIDE TO FINDING
A JOB YOU LOVE

HEATHER HUND

ISBN-10: 0692133305
ISBN-13: 978-0692133309

DEDICATION

To my son – and the next generation

CONTENTS

ART

of the

JOB SEARCH

INTRODUCTION

CHANGE YOUR LIFE

Do you want to find a job you love? A role where you like the work? A place where you like the culture and the people around you? A position where you're learning, having an impact—and doing what you love?

But perhaps you aren't sure what you want to do next? Or how to create a resume that leads to interviews—or how to network, interview or negotiate? Or maybe all these things?

Five years ago, I left my job—without another one. When I first took the job, I loved the weekly travel and exploring new cities across the country. But, a year into the role, something changed: I got married. Suddenly, getting on a plane every Sunday night was no longer quite as appealing.

So, I decided that it was time to make a change. I wanted to be intentional and find a job I would love—but wasn't quite sure how to do it. During my time at Stanford Business School, I applied for tons of internships and received only one offer. At the time, I wondered: *How did some people have so many offers at places they really wanted to work?*

Turns out, they knew something that I didn't at the time: the *art* of the job search.

People often think that others with certain degrees or companies on their resumes are guaranteed success. Luckily, this is not the case. You do *not* need a 4.0 GPA or the perfect background to find a job you love. All you need is the knowledge of how to search—and the understanding that it's about finding the right *match*.

To find a job I would love, I started by interviewing people who had done it. How did they figure out what they wanted to do? How did they approach networking? Specifically, what questions did they ask? How did they prepare for interviews? What were their tips for interviewing? How did they negotiate? Did it work? And how did they think about their career—and even more importantly, their life?

One of the most important things I learned was that success is not getting all the jobs for which you apply, the most prestigious position or the highest salary. Instead, success is finding a job you love—where you enjoy going to work most days, like the people around you and are excited about the work you're doing. It's working at a place where you feel like you can be yourself—and not like you have to be someone else to succeed. In short:

Job search success is simply this: finding the right *match*.

I admired the people I knew who had done this—they seemed so much happier and successful. So, I resolved to:

1. Learn how to job search *effectively*
2. Seek the right *match*

To do these things, I realized that I would need to take a radically different approach than I had in the past. Instead of scouring websites and applying for anything that looked remotely interesting, I started by figuring out what types of jobs I would want to do. (You can do the same by taking the self-assessment in Chapter 2.)

Then, I implemented what I learned about how to conduct a strategic job search, which corresponds to the eleven steps in this book.

This time, I received six offers—out of the eight positions I interviewed for. And most importantly, I loved the job I ended up taking.

Finding the right match will almost always involve hearing no—and more often, hearing nothing at all. I applied to many more jobs but didn't make it to the interview phase. I was switching industries, and not everyone was convinced that I had enough experience in the new field. Several companies never got back to me at all after I submitted my resume. (I later learned that this is *very* common—more on this in Chapter 3.)

When these things happen, they are simply an indication that you are willing to put yourself out there in pursuit of a higher goal, which is brave—very brave. Just because someone tells you "no" doesn't mean they're right. Instead of giving up, see what you can learn—and then apply it.

By being willing to endure rejection, I found a job that I loved. The work was interesting, my manager was amazing—and I really liked the team. This position also enabled me to have the life that I wanted outside of work. I took painting classes with a friend, cooked dinner with my husband several times a week, saw my friends more often—and finally got a puppy. (Ollie is now a full-grown Golden Retriever, and he's been a great addition to our lives.)

Doing work you love can bring more than just personal fulfillment. At my new company, I was promoted twice and received three raises over two years. In my prior job, neither of these things had happened. Coincidence? Probably not. Research indicates that loving your job also leads to greater success.

You might be wondering: were there tradeoffs? As with most

major life decisions: yes. The biggest tradeoff I made was salary trajectory. My starting salary was similar, but in five years, I likely wouldn't earn as much. For me, the tradeoff at this time in my life was worth it—and I negotiated my starting salary to be 20 percent higher than the original offer using the approach discussed in Chapter 10.

Through my experience, I realized something critical: there is an *art* to the job search—especially when you are trying to live intentionally and find work you love. And even more importantly, I learned this:

You can love your work, and life is so much better when you do.

Below are the most important things to consider in designing your career.

4 TRUTHS ABOUT FINDING A JOB YOU LOVE

1. You can find work you love.
Often, we think that our options are limited to positions in our current industry or only to the jobs that come our way. This simply isn't true. You can switch industries, change roles, or start your own business. Admittedly, these things often take more work and time, but you can do them if you really want to.

2. You will be happier, and usually more successful, in a position you love.
The average person spends 60% of their waking weekday hours at work. So, it's not surprising that research indicates that liking your work leads to greater happiness—and more career success, like more frequent raises and promotions.

3. You don't need to know exactly what you want to do.

4

Often, we feel like we can't change jobs because we don't know what we want to do next. But you don't need to know *exactly* what you want to do next to start your search. Most of us will have fourteen to twenty different jobs over our lives. Instead of trying to find the perfect job, focus on moving in the right direction. Start by taking the self-assessment in Chapter 2.

4. A job is only great if it's a match on both sides.
Even when you conduct a strategic job search, as outlined in this book, you won't get every position. That's okay. Sometimes, it's not a match, as discussed in Chapter 3. But when you do find your match, it can be amazing.

11 STEPS TO FIND A JOB YOU LOVE

Did you know:
- Networking leads to 85% of jobs (not online resume drops).
- 50% of all jobs are *not* posted online.
- Failing to negotiate $5k in your first job can lead to lost earnings of $500k+ over your life.

These statistics illustrate an important reality: the job search is not straightforward. Take the first scenario, the application process. Most people apply to jobs online even though networking is much more likely to be effective. Later in this book, we will discuss how to network and apply in a way that will give you a better chance of getting an interview.

This book provides a step-by-step approach to getting more interviews, better offers—and most importantly, a job you love. Specifically, we will take an eleven-step approach, which includes how to:

- Figure out what you want to do next
- Build the confidence to search

- Create an amazing resume
- Network authentically (even if you're an introvert)
- Interview effectively
- Negotiate and make $500k in your lifetime
- Set yourself up for success in your new job

Throughout my career at companies including Goldman Sachs, Boston Consulting Group, and Gap, Inc., I have interviewed numerous candidates and reviewed hundreds of resumes. For this book, I also interviewed people at companies like Google, Facebook, and other Fortune 100 companies in addition to people at smaller companies—from hedge funds to non-profits to startups.

These conversations provided insight into how hiring works across different companies—and what to do in various scenarios. Why would a company not follow up after you submit your resume online? Why would they not call you after an interview? And most importantly, what you can do if these things happen?

As you use this book, remember that you are learning and developing new skills that you will use throughout your career—and life. Often, people think that skills like negotiating are innate, but this perspective couldn't be further from the truth. These things are learned and improved with practice, just like anything in life—from meditating to learning Japanese.

Be patient as you learn, and remember that you are building new skills—ones that will enable you to design a career you love over your lifetime.

HOW THIS BOOK CAN HELP YOU

Until recently, people had one or two jobs during their lives. They chose a company early in their career and stayed. Then, after forty years, they retired happily ever after. But, the world has changed since then—quite a bit.

Today, most of us will have fourteen jobs over the course of our careers. And if you are a millennial, you will likely have over twenty different roles throughout your career. Given that you will likely be changing roles every two to five years, learning how to job search is critical to create a career you love.

A job search is an opportunity. You get to take the time to figure out what you want to do next and what you want to contribute to the world—and along the way, develop skills that will enable you to build a career you love over your lifetime.

Regardless of where you are in your career, this book can help. If you are:

- **In School:** This book can help you learn how to find jobs you love over the course of your career—even for your first job or internship.

- **Employed:** Before you start applying, try to invest the time to read this book to 1) figure out what you want to do next and 2) learn how to effectively search, which will help ensure that you find the right next role for you.

- **Unemployed:** You are free to find a job you love—and this book can help. If your finances allow, take the time to find the right next job, versus taking whatever comes next. If you need income while you search, you could try to find consulting gigs or part-time work.

To get the most out of this book, use it however it's most helpful for you. If you have time, I recommend reading it from cover to cover first. Then, reread each chapter during each specific phase of your job search. But if you have a big interview in two days and are short on time, go ahead and jump to the interview chapter. This book can be useful regardless of where you are in your search, whether you've just started or are looking to negotiate an offer.

Additionally, this book is intended to provide guidance. Often, people don't know how to write networking emails, what questions to ask while networking, or how to answer interview questions.

This book includes specific guidance, like email examples and lists of networking and interview questions, but try to make these your own when you can. Each interaction and relationship is different, so approach them in a way that feels authentic and genuine to you. So, write your own emails. Go off-script during a networking call. The best interactions are usually the unscripted ones. This book simply provides guidance—lots of it—but the key is to make it authentically your own.

For some helpful resources, check out the website, http://www.artofthejobsearch.co/. It includes all the resources referenced in this book under Free Resources. These include a sample resume and cover letter, a resume template, a negotiation calculator, top interview questions—and more.

Above all, remember this:

You can find a job you love—and create the life you want.

1. THE FIRST STEP

YOU CAN FIND A JOB YOU LOVE

Have you ever had a job where you felt fulfilled? Where you knew you were making an impact? Where you felt supported by your manager? Where you liked the people around you? Where you were often learning? Where you could create the life outside of work that you wanted?

Lots of people have not ever had this experience, so doubt that something like this could exist for them—but it can.

Finding a job you love can be life-changing.

From the outside, Alex had the perfect job. But, most days, he came home drained by the eighty-hour weeks and intense culture. So, he decided to make a change.

He ultimately found a small company in a space he was passionate about: music. While his income was initially half of what he made in his prior role, he loved his job and the life it enabled him to create. He enjoyed working with bands, the great team, having more time to spend with his girlfriend, family and friends—not to mention being able to walk to his office in five minutes.

Seven years later, he's now the CEO of the company—and continues to love his job most days.

So, what does it mean to find a job you love?

- Being **interested in your work**
- **Liking the people**
- Feeling like you can **be yourself**
- **Feeling supported** and **valued**
- **Learning** in your job
- **Creating the life you want** outside work

Even in a job you love, not everything will be perfect. Maybe you have to do a couple hours of reporting each week, work with some people you don't like, or empty your own trash every day. You may even encounter some larger challenges or disappointments.

After working at a large company for several years, Noah joined a smaller firm in a more entrepreneurial role—and he loved it. In his new role, he got to build a new business and a relationship with the CEO. His manager was so impressed by his performance that he promised Noah a promotion at the end of the year—but it didn't happen. While he was disappointed, Noah stayed and decided to talk to senior leaders to get feedback—and this approach paid off. He was promoted the next year and became the youngest partner at the company—at the age of 31.

If you do encounter large challenges in your job, try to look at the bigger picture. Do you feel like you're moving in the right direction? Are you still learning? Are you still enjoying working with the people? Is this setback highly detrimental to your career? (It's usually not.)

So, how are you feeling about your current job? When you think about your current role, how do you feel? Unhappy? Overwhelmed? Overworked? Bored? Underutilized? Like your career has stagnated—or soon will? Stressed? Or, just that it's time to make a change?

According to a recent study, up to 80 percent of people are unhappy at work, yet only 20 percent are planning to look for a new job.

People think they can't find a job they love for all kinds of reasons—because they didn't go to Harvard or Yale or because they don't have Google or Facebook on their resume. But usually these things are *not* required.

Your world of opportunity is probably so much larger than you imagine.

When my friend Eva decided to change jobs, she found her dream startup. When she looked at the team online, she noticed something: everyone who worked there had a PhD from a top school—Harvard, Stanford, Princeton, Dartmouth. But Eva didn't have a PhD or an Ivy League degree.

Many people would have stopped there. But Eva decided to find someone in her network who worked at the company and have coffee with them. During their conversation, she shared her enthusiasm for the company and her knowledge about the industry—and ultimately got an interview. (This is how effective networking works—more in Chapter 5.)

She put a ton of work into the interview preparations, spending over fifteen hours on the required project—and got the job.

As her story illustrates, you don't need certain degrees or companies on your resume to get your dream job, even if others at the company have these qualifications. Passion, knowledge, and effort can go a long way.

LOVING YOUR WORK = MORE HAPPINESS & SUCCESS

After only a year in her job, Pia was burned out by the long hours and travel. Then, she learned that she was not on track for promotion. While she was initially devastated, she realized that she had a choice: work even harder for a promotion *or* move on to something else. She ultimately decided to leave—and find a job she loved.

In her new position, Pia loved her work, the culture and her colleagues—and was promoted three times in only five years. Coincidence? Probably not. According to research, being happy at work can lead to more success.

Recent research reveals that people who are happy in their jobs:

- Get **promoted** more frequently
- **Earn more**
- Get **more support**
- Generate more **creative ideas**
- **Achieve goals** faster
- **Interact better** with colleagues and bosses
- Receive **higher reviews**
- **Learn** more
- Achieve **greater success**
- Are **healthier**

In short, being happy in your job can lead to more opportunities, higher performance and better health, which are all pretty great things.

HOW TO MAKE A MAJOR CAREER CHANGE

Often, people want to make a major career change—but feel like it's impossible. I have made several changes in my career, which includes private equity, consulting, retail strategy—in addition to art investing, education reform work and startup consulting.

My hypothesis is that the world is changing—and that many companies will seek generalists and people who can learn to do the role, versus people with years of experience doing the same type of work. But in our world today, what I've found is that people often measure your potential based on your past (specifically what's on your resume). However, that doesn't mean that it's impossible to make a major career change.

What I have found is that the easiest way to make a change is to leverage skills you already have. When I left strategy consulting with the goal of working in retail operations, I started by joining the strategy team in a new industry: retail. Then, a year later, I shifted into a new role at Gap that was operational—and enabled me to build a new team.

It is possible to make an even bigger change and usually requires showing the company what you can do *and* finding someone who believes in you and is willing to take a chance on you. Those people are out there—you just must find them.

If you aim to make a major career change, the following approach can be helpful.

THE 4 CAREER CHANGE STEPS

1. Figure out what it will take.
This requires networking to figure out two things.

1. *What does the job you want entail?* It's easy to idealize something without understanding what it *really* is.
2. *What is required to make the switch?* You will probably receive some different answers to this question—that's common, as people often take different paths to get to the same place. So, try to talk to several people. (You can use the networking approach in Chapter 5.)

2. Decide what you are willing to do.

Once you get an idea of what it would take, ask yourself: are you willing to do it? There was a point in my career where I was interested in working in merchandising—I talked to several people and kept hearing that I would need to start at the bottom. At that point, I was almost ten years into my career and didn't want to take that many steps back. Instead, I took a role that worked directly with merchandising teams, which helped me gain the knowledge that I sought.

3. Gain the knowledge and experience you need.

Your networking discussions will help you figure out what you need to do. Here are some ideas of how to gain knowledge in a new space:

- **Read.** Before you even start networking, start reading. Read books. Read articles. Subscribe to industry newsletters. (You can ask people on your networking calls which industry newsletters they recommend.) Search for relevant articles on Medium or use Google to see if anyone has aggregated resources.

- **Do a project or get an internship.** Doing work in the space will help build your credibility and show your commitment to making a career change. If you can, try to find work at a place you want to work full-time—and offer to work there for free, on a project or on a short-term basis. Doing your best work can lead to an offer—or the experience you need to break into the industry. Multiple people have shared stories of doing this. My favorite is that of a friend who wanted an investment banking internship during his junior year in college—but didn't get an offer. So, he called one of the firms and offered to work for the summer—for free. They took him up on it—and at the end of the summer, he was the only intern who got a full time offer. His story goes to show that taking initiative can go a very long way.

- **Take a course at a local college.** Most colleges offer continuing education classes, which are often the same classes that students take. A friend recently told me she emailed her alma mater and asked to sit in on classes she's interested in—they agreed, and it's free.

- **Take an online course.** Another great option is an online course. There are all kinds of places you can do this. Coursera offers online courses from top universities. Lynda offers courses from experts. Bloc offers coding and software development courses. Seth Godin's AltMBA is a great four-week alternative to the traditional MBA. And then there are some free specialized resources like Khan Academy and Code Academy. YouTube can also be an interesting source of knowledge.

- **Go to conferences.** These can be a *great* way to gain knowledge and to make personal connections in a new industry. Ask others you know in the industry which conferences they recommend.

- **Get a coach.** Often, it's helpful to have someone support you through a career change. To find a coach, start with your network. In the past, I sent an email to about thirty friends to get recommendations. Before you hire a coach, have an initial chat with the coaches you are considering to see if it's a good fit. Great coaches help guide you, usually through insightful questions—not by providing answers or telling you what to do with your life.

4. Continue to network. Making a major career change requires finding someone who is willing to take a chance on you, since you likely won't have all the experience required. To find these people, usually even more networking is required. So, network—a lot.

Making a big career change usually requires more work. But if you really want something, why not try it? You only have one life to live, after all. And if you don't know what you want to do next, you're in good company. Most people aren't sure what they want to do at the beginning of their job search. Chapter 2 can help you identify your path.

A LAYOFF IS AN OPPORTUNITY

After creating the wildly successful Macintosh computer, Steve Jobs was essentially fired from Apple, the very company whose success he arguably created. As anyone would be, he was initially distraught, stating, "What had been the focus of my entire adult life was gone, and it was devastating." He added, "I was a very public failure."

Instead of retreating from the public eye, Jobs turned his layoff into an opportunity. He went on to develop another company, co-founding Pixar Animation Studios and creating classic movies like *Toy Story* and *Finding Nemo*.

Of his layoff and rebound, Jobs later said:

> *It turned out that getting fired from Apple was the best thing that could have ever happened to me. The heaviness of being successful was replaced by the lightness of being a beginner again, less sure about everything. It freed me to enter one of the most creative periods of my life.*

> *I'm pretty sure none of this would have happened if I hadn't been fired from Apple. It was awful tasting medicine, but I guess the patient needed it. Sometimes life hits you in the head with a brick. Don't lose faith. I'm convinced the only thing that kept me going was that I loved what I did.* **You've got to find what you love.**

As Steve Jobs learned, a job change can be a catalyst to do something amazing in your career and life—something you love that might even change the world.

HOW TO BEGIN YOUR SEARCH

Here are some common questions on how to begin your search:

Should you quit your job to search?

It depends. If you have the financial means, quitting your job can give you more time to devote to your job search. Have you ever heard the saying, "job searching is a full-time job?" It's a cliché, because it can be true—a job search can require a lot of work.

Finding the right position can take a lot of time—in my experience, up to six months, or even a year. So, if you choose to take time off to job search, ensure that you've saved enough to cover your financial needs for at least a year, and ideally more.

Should you take time between jobs?

Leaving your job can also enable you to fulfill personal passions. Recently, my husband and I left our jobs to pursue our dreams: we lived in a mountain town for a ski season, road tripped through the American West, and traveled through Africa. It was amazing—and required some serious financial planning, including saving for years, renting our home, and budgeting for our expenses. Realizing that it could take time to find new jobs, we ensured that we had saved enough to cover at least a year of job searching *after* our travels ended.

I often get asked this question: what happens if interviewers don't understand your time off? What I have discovered is that most people don't even ask about gaps on a resume. But even if they do, you have a great story to share. Tell them about how you took time off to spend with your kids or how you fulfilled your life dream of attending cooking school in France.

And if your interviewers don't understand, do you want to work with people who don't value life outside of work?

How do you conduct a search if you are still employed?

Trying to balance a job search with work can be challenging, so set realistic goals for yourself. You could aim to network with two people a week on the phone, which will mean that at the end of the month, you will have networked with eight people.

Another important thing is to ensure that you prioritize your job search. Often, people say, "I really want to change jobs but don't have time to search." Think of your overall life and career objectives, and prioritize accordingly. It may require devoting less time to current work projects or saying "no" more often.

Should you tell your employer you are searching?

It depends. If you are interested in other roles within the company, discuss it with your manager. A recommendation from your manager is usually required to interview for roles within the same company. Even if you prefer to stay at your current company, it can be beneficial to interview for roles *outside* of your company. You may not find a position at your company. And if you do, outside offers will give you more leverage in your negotiations.

If you are not interested in staying at your current company, it may not make sense to tell your employer that you are searching, unless it is common practice at your company. People often worry that their coworkers will notice that they are gone for interviews. How often do you notice when someone is not at their desk? You are probably too busy most days to think about whether they are at the dentist or an interview. (That said, if you do put outside interviews on your calendar, mark them as "private appointment.")

2. THE SELF-ASSESSMENT

NO PLAN? NO PROBLEM.

Unlike most people who change jobs every few years, Sophia has had the same job for eleven years—and she likes it. I always wondered how she knew *exactly* what she wanted to do just two years out of college?

When I finally asked Sophia that question, her answer surprised me: "I didn't."

Through a longer discussion, I learned that she *did* have very specific criteria in her job search. She determined what she liked and disliked in all her prior jobs and internships, identified her strengths and weaknesses—and targeted positions accordingly. She also defined the culture she wanted—one where people did not take themselves too seriously, prioritized family, and enjoyed life outside of work.

Figuring out what she wanted and developing general criteria before she started her search enabled Sophia to find a match so great that she's stayed—for eleven years.

In short, you don't need to know *exactly* what you want to do when you decide to make a career change, but it can be helpful to have criteria.

Many people hesitate to start a job search, and often stay in jobs they dislike, simply because they don't have an answer to, "So . . . what do you want to do next?" Admittedly, it can be stressful to get this question when you don't have a clear answer. But here's the thing:

You don't need to know *exactly* what you want to do next to start your job search.

The beauty of a job search is just that: it's a *search*—meaning that it's all about exploration. You don't need to know what you want to do when you start. Instead, start by determining what you want to *explore* using the self-assessment below.

This will be useful for the next step: networking, which can help you figure out what you want to do. Through networking, you will likely discover new interests, intriguing roles or fascinating companies that you didn't know existed. (Know now that effective networking probably isn't what you think it is—and does *not* involve wandering around hotel conference rooms wearing a sticky nametag. Read Chapter 5 before you start networking to learn how to do it in an authentic, effective and enjoyable way).

THE SELF-ASSESSMENT: 5 QUESTIONS TO FIND YOUR PATH

Before you start applying to jobs, take the self-assessment on the following pages first, which can help you figure out what *you* want to target in your search—not what your parents, friends, or anyone else think you should do. Or even what you think you *should* do. Remember that there are no universally best jobs—only the best ones for you.

The exercise below will take you through a series of self-assessments related to five big-picture questions:

1. What do you like and dislike in a job?
2. What type of culture do you seek?
3. What are your strengths and weaknesses?
4. What are your goals (personal, professional, financial)?
5. What are your deal-breakers?

As you go through the exercise, write down your answers to the questions. You can find an example at the end of this chapter.

There is also a downloadable Self-Assessment worksheet on the *Art of the Job Search* website under <u>Free Resources</u>.

Keep your completed self-assessment with you throughout your search, and reference it during each step of the process to ensure that it's aligned with what you're seeking. And, remember:

A job is only right when it's a *match* on both sides.

PART 1:
WHAT DO YOU LIKE AND DISLIKE IN A JOB?

"Do what you love, and you'll never have to work another day in your life."
—Unknown, but unquestionably true

Too often, career choices are driven by things we feel like we should do. "I *should* be an engineer, because my uncle says it's a good job." Or, "I *should* work in technology, because everyone else wants to." "I *should* work in whatever job, because it pays well/would set me up well for a future job/would look good on my resume, etc."

Identifying what you like and dislike at work can prevent you from making decisions based on what you think you should do. Because working in a job *you* want to do can lead to much greater success—and happiness.

After six years of working in fashion, Chloe came home one day and realized that it was time to make a change. By starting with a self-assessment, she realized that she loved entrepreneurship and design—and ultimately decided to establish her own interior design business. Seven years later, Chloe still loves her work, at least on most days.

For the exercise below, think about all the jobs you've had in the past. What did you specifically like and dislike in these roles? Don't worry about being organized. Write whatever comes to mind. If you are still in school, consider your subjects and classes, and hypothesize about what you might like and dislike in a job.

The questions below are intended as a starting point. You do not need to answer every question, and if you have thoughts outside of these questions, include those as well. Record your answers on your Self-Assessment worksheet.

QUESTIONS TO ASK YOURSELF
(LIKES/ DISLIKES)

Types of work
- What tasks do you like/dislike (e.g., writing, presentations, influencing, data analysis, coding, solving problems, negotiating, etc.)?
- What types of work do you like/dislike (e.g., strategy, analytics, marketing, sales, etc.)?

Industries
- What industries are you interested in? If you don't know, consider these questions:
  - What subjects do you enjoy reading about in the news (e.g., retail, healthcare, technology)?
  - What academic subjects do you like and dislike?
  - What do you like learning about?

Company & Team Dynamics

- Do you like primarily working alone, with others, or a mix?
- Do you like working at big, small, or mid-sized companies?
- Do you like being a part of a big or small team?
- Do you like managing and developing people? If so, what size teams?

Other

- Do you like working with clients? Customers?
- What did you love the most in prior jobs?
- What drove you crazy at prior jobs?

EXAMPLE
(LIKES/ DISLIKES)

Write down the things you enjoyed most and least in your past jobs, internships, or studies.

Likes	Dislikes
Strategy	Optimizing processes
Working with people	Hierarchy
Building things	Doing the same thing everyday
Developing people	Client work
Healthcare	
Managing small teams (2-5 people)	

PART 2:
WHAT TYPE OF CULTURE DO YOU SEEK?

Culture. It's such a buzzword these days, but what is a good culture? In my opinion, it's simple: finding a place where you agree with the values and can be yourself at work—and still succeed.

Research indicates that cultural fit leads to greater job

satisfaction, longer tenure, and better performance.

Culture can make a huge difference in how you feel about your job.

Think about how good it feels to work in a place where you feel comfortable—and have friends. According to recent research conducted by Gallup, "close work friendships boost work satisfaction by 50 percent."

In her first job, Sienna thought the work was interesting but didn't feel connected with her co-workers. When she decided to make a switch, she prioritized culture—and found a company with people she liked. She made several friends at work, and seven years later, they have attended each other's weddings—and now go on an annual camping trip in Yosemite.

It's easy to idealize a company without considering whether you would like the culture—but, think carefully about culture. It can be immensely challenging to work at a place where you feel like you need to be someone else to succeed, or where you disagree with the values.

While it can be hard to put words on the intangible thing known as culture, the exercise below aims to help you start to think about it—and what you would ideally want.

QUESTIONS TO ASK YOURSELF
(CULTURE)

What kind of culture would you want? Here's an example:

I am seeking a culture where people:
- Value the career advancement of women
- Are collaborative and friendly
- View taking risks as learning, not failure

- Are mission-driven and believe in what they are doing
- Prioritize life outside of work

Often, it can be hard to define what you seek in a culture, so you could start with this list of words used to define culture.

Examples include:

- Autonomous
- Collaborative
- Competitive
- Conservative
- Flat
- Flexible
- Formal
- Friendly
- Hierarchical
- Informal
- Relaxed
- Risk Taking
- Structured
- Unstructured

EXAMPLE
(CULTURE)

What do you like and dislike in a culture?

Like	Dislike
Autonomous	Rigid
Flat	Formal
Informal	Competitive
Collaborative	
Friendly	

Innovative	

I am seeking a culture where people:

- Seek diverse opinions
- Celebrate failure
- Are less formal and can be themselves
- Value strategy as a function
- Prioritize life outside of work

PART 3:
WHAT ARE YOUR STRENGTHS AND WEAKNESSES?

When you receive feedback, what do you focus on more: fixing your weaknesses or further building your strengths? If you're like most people, you focus on fixing your weaknesses.

However, modern research reveals that true greatness is achieved by taking the opposite approach: building your strengths. A leadership firm, Zenger Folkman, found that exceptional leaders are "really outstanding at doing a few things well." So instead of trying to fix all your weaknesses, focus on building your unique strengths. Note these words: *a few*. Focus on developing just two or three key strengths, not several.

Below, identify your strengths. What do you excel at? What sets you apart? In your next role, try to find a job where you utilize—and continue to build—your key strengths. Conversely, avoid roles where a primary component of the job involves a major weakness. For example, if negotiating is a weakness, a sales role is probably not right for you.

To identify your strengths and weaknesses, consider past feedback that you have received at work and in your personal life. If you haven't received much feedback, ask your coworkers (past or present) and honest friends for feedback.

You may have received conflicting feedback over the course of your career. This is common. It's possible that you have corrected a weakness or that the feedback is incorrect. Remember that feedback is just one person's point of view. Try to identify themes, and trust your intuition.

QUESTIONS TO ASK YOURSELF
(STRENGTHS/ WEAKNESSES)

What are your strengths? What are your weaknesses? Below are some examples, but you don't need to limit yourself to this list. This is simply a starting point. Include feedback you have received and things you know about yourself.

Examples include:

- Communication – written or verbal
- Consensus building
- Creativity
- Data analysis
- Influencing
- Innovation
- Management
- Negotiating
- Prioritization
- Process optimization
- Solving problems
- Strategy

Once you've completed this exercise, highlight the two strengths that you: 1) most want to further develop in your next job and 2) really enjoy doing.

EXAMPLE
(STRENGTHS/ WEAKNESSES)

What are your key strengths? What are your primary weaknesses? After you have written these down, highlight the two strengths that you: 1) want to further develop in your next job and 2) enjoy.

Strengths	Weaknesses
Strategy	Negotiation
Growing businesses	Optimizing processes
Working cross-functionally	
Communication	
Developing people	

PART 4:
WHAT ARE YOUR GOALS?

Recently, I asked a good friend about his long-term goals. He's one of the most impressive people I know, with a diverse background that includes teaching at a public school in Baltimore, creating his own educational startup, and working at a top tech company. Given his experience, I wondered how he thought about the future. How does he set long-term goals?

His answer was thought-provoking: he doesn't.

What he's realized is that you learn more about yourself with each experience—what you like, what you don't like, what you want out of your next experience, and how to make it work with what's going on in your life.

Recently, he had triplets. This was a bit of a surprise—an exciting one that changed his goals. Financially supporting his family rose to the top of the list, followed by personal growth and having an impact through his work. These priorities make his current job at a stable, top tech company the right one—for now.

QUESTIONS TO ASK YOURSELF
(GOALS – CAREER, PERSONAL & FINANCIAL)

Career Goals

Short-Term Career Goals:

Overall, what do you seek in your next job? Identify two to three goals, at most. Research indicates that people can only focus on a few goals at one time. If you are not sure what your goals are, ask yourself the following questions:

- Is there a skill you want to further develop (e.g., manage people, present to senior leaders, manage a budget)?
- Is there knowledge you aim to acquire (e.g., marketing, coding, manufacturing)?
- Is there industry expertise you want to gain (e.g., retail, healthcare, technology)?
- Is there a strength you want to further cultivate?

Long-Term Career Goals:

You don't need to be specific, as your long-term goals will likely change throughout your career as you learn more about yourself. Additionally, jobs are changing as the world does. You might have a job in five years that does not yet exist.

Personal Goals

One of my favorite managers had the following mantra: "We work to live, not live to work." Finding a job that will enable you to pursue your personal goals can lead to greater overall fulfillment.

What do you want to do outside of work?

- Spend time with friends/family?
- Pursue hobbies?
- Exercise?
- Volunteer?
- Travel?

Research indicates that work/life balance is a strong predictor of happiness, but what constitutes work/life balance is different for everyone. What's most important is figuring out what you want.

When you get to the point of assessing specific opportunities, ask yourself the following questions:

- Will this job allow you to pursue your personal goals?
- If not, how important are these things to your happiness?
- Can you change anything about the job to align it with your personal goals?

Financial Goals

Should money be a factor in your career decisions? Yes—and no. It's important to determine the salary necessary to support yourself, your family, and your life. But targeting jobs solely because of salary likely will not lead to satisfaction. Research indicates that salary does not correlate to happiness above $75,000.

Which friend do you admire most—the one who makes the most money? Or the one who really loves their work? There's something about the person who *loves* their job.

Envision the life you want and the things you want to do, and estimate your annual expenses, like housing, food, insurance, travel, donations, savings, and hobbies. Quantify each of these things and make a financial plan to figure out what salary you need.

Ask yourself:
- What is the minimum salary you need to support yourself and your family? (Online budgeting tools, like Mint, can be helpful.)

EXAMPLE
(GOALS – CAREER, PERSONAL & FINANCIAL)

Professional Goals	Personal Goals	Financial Goals

Next Job: • Manage people • Build presentation skills • Learn the solar industry	Quality time with family (nightly dinners + weekends)	Min Salary: $90,000
Long Term: Become a digital marketing expert	Time for hobbies, including yoga 3x per week	

PART 5:
WHAT ARE YOUR DEAL-BREAKERS?

Elena got an offer that she really wanted to take, but it required a three-hour daily commute. Despite her friends' stories of how they enjoyed listening to podcasts or calling friends on their long commutes, she knew how much she disliked driving. So, she turned down the offer. A long commute was a deal-breaker for her.

There's an inherent tradeoff in honoring deal-breakers. Since they are meant to limit the jobs you would take (or even apply for), think carefully about what your deal-breakers are.

Should you apply to jobs that violate deal-breakers? Yes, but *only* if you think it's possible to negotiate a deal-breaker. Sara only applied to full-time jobs, even though she only wanted to work four days a week so she could spend Fridays at home with her young daughter. When Sara received offers, she negotiated to work four days a week with full-time pay and benefits—and got to spend each Friday with her daughter.

To determine your deal-breakers, ask yourself the following questions:

QUESTIONS TO ASK YOURSELF
(DEAL-BREAKERS)

Hours:

- What are the hours that you are willing to work?
- Do you want to be home at a certain time each day?
- Do you prefer a flexible schedule?
- Are you okay working nights and/or weekends?
- Do you want to work from home at all (e.g. one day a week)?

Commute:

- How long are you willing to commute each day?
- If you commute, are you okay driving, taking a bus, train, biking, or walking?

Travel:

- Are you willing to travel in a job?
- If yes, how much are you willing to do?
- Are you willing to travel internationally?

EXAMPLE
(DEAL-BREAKERS)

What are your deal-breakers (i.e., reasons you would not take a job)?
- Commute (more than 1 hour each way)
- Travel (more than 5 days per month)
- Hours (more than 50 per week)

HOW TO IDENTIFY JOBS YOU WANT

The next step is to use the information above to determine what industries, functions and companies you want to explore through networking. See below for how to think about these things.

INDUSTRIES OF INTEREST

Start by identifying what industries you want to explore further. You can explore more than one industry, so if you're interested in healthcare, education, and retail, add them all to your list.

Reference the list of industries below, and ask yourself the following questions:

- What industries and topics do you like learning about (e.g., news, podcasts, blogs)?
- What industries would you want to read about?
- Would you enjoy discussing the industry with colleagues?
- Would you care enough to have opinions about the industry (e.g., hypothesize with a colleague about the future of the industry)?

Here is a list of potential industries. While it is not comprehensive, it provides a good starting point:

Accounting, Audit, and Taxes
Advertising, Marketing, and PR
Agriculture
Arts
Consumer
Education
Energy
Financial Services
Government
Healthcare
HR and Recruiting
Investment Banking
Legal Services
Management Consulting
Manufacturing
Media and Entertainment
Non-profit
Private Equity

Real Estate
Retail
Technology
Telecommunications
Travel, Recreation, and Leisure
Venture Capital

Write down your industries of interest. You can, and likely will, add more as you network.

FUNCTIONS OF INTEREST

For the next step, start thinking what type of job functions you want to further explore. See below for a list. Based on what you currently know, what functions seem interesting and aligned with your strengths and interests?

At this point, keep an open mind. During your networking conversations, you may discover jobs that you didn't know existed. Record the functions you are interested in exploring—and remember, they are just a starting place. Continue to add to your list as you network.

Here is a list of potential functions. While it is not comprehensive, it provides a good starting place:

Accounting
Analytics & Data Science
Business Development
Design
Engineering
Finance
Human Resources
Information Technology
Legal
Marketing
Operations

Product Management
Project Management
Public Relations
Research
Sales
Social Impact
Strategy

COMPANIES OF INTEREST

At this point, do you have any companies that you would like to further explore when you network? If so, write them in Column B of your <u>Networking Tracker</u>. We will revisit this in Chapter 5, where you will learn how to find people who work at these companies. Your list of companies will also likely grow as you begin networking and learn more about your industries of interest.

BEYOND ALGORITHMS

So, what do you do with all this information? Wouldn't it be nice if there was an algorithm that could take your data and give you the perfect match? There probably will be something like this in the future, perhaps even soon, but I'm not aware of anything accurate yet. What tests and algorithms neglect to account for is something critically important: the people.

Job searching is a lot like dating. You might find a job that looks great on paper but when you interview, you realize that the culture is all wrong.

So, here's what this exercise should do: help you identify your strengths, what you like—and what you would like to avoid. And it should give you a better idea of what you want to explore in the next critical step: networking.

SELF-ASSESSMENT: FIND A JOB YOU *LOVE*

Complete this exercise to determine what to look for in your next job.
Remember: a job is only right when it's a match on both sides.

1. LIKES & DISLIKES

Write down the things you enjoyed most and least in all your past jobs, internships
(or studies if you are still in school).

Likes	Dislikes

2. CULTURE

What would you like and dislike in a culture?

Likes	Dislikes

I am seeking a culture where people:

-
-
-

3. STRENGTHS & WEAKNESSES

What are your key strengths? What are your primary weaknesses? Last, highlight
the two strengths that you most: 1) want to further develop in your next job and

2) enjoy.

Strengths	Weaknesses

4. GOALS

What are your career goals – both in your next job and long term? How about your personal and financial goals?

Career Goals	Personal Goals	Financial Goals
Next Job:		Min Salary:
Long Term:		

5. DEAL BREAKERS

What are your deal-breakers (e.g. reasons you could not take a job?)

1.

2.

3.

NEXT STEPS: INDUSTRIES, FUNCTIONS & COMPANIES

Rank these if you can, and continue to add to this list as you discover more areas of interest throughout your job search process.

Industries	Functions	Companies

3. MINDSET

THERE IS NO SUCH THING AS FAILURE

Before the start of business school, I travelled to Colombia with some classmates. On a plane ride from Cartagena to Bogota, I sat next to someone I had never met. During the conversation, he asked me where I had worked before school, and I mentioned that I had been at a startup for the past year.

He asked the inevitable question, "What's the company called?"

I paused and then confessed that it had failed. His response shocked me. He smiled and said, "That's awesome!" Then, he asked me a very insightful question, "What did you learn?"

No one had ever asked me that before, and the truth was that I had learned all kinds of things. I learned what worked in low-budget email marketing—and what didn't. I learned that working with the right team is often more important than the work itself. I learned that I must be passionate about my work to be at my best.

After discussing this in depth, he said words I will never forget, "See, you didn't fail. You learned."

And he was right: just because something doesn't work out like you hoped doesn't mean you failed. You almost always learn something on your journey, which will ultimately take you where you need to be. And when you learn something, there's no such thing as failure.

So, throughout your search, especially when setbacks happen, remember:

You're learning—and there's something *amazing* out there for you.

When setbacks happen, it means that you are taking steps to find something you really love—and that you are brave enough to put yourself out there.

Rejection doesn't determine your worth. After all, a job is only right when it's a *match* on both sides. Sometimes it's not a match—and something better is out there waiting for you. Admittedly, it's hard to feel this way when you don't know what the next thing is, but have faith that there's something out there for you. And be nice to yourself when things don't turn out like you hoped.

Remember that success is not getting every job for which you apply. Instead, it's having the courage to put yourself out there to try to find a job you would really like. That's brave—and will lead to lots of learnings along the way that will ultimately help you find a job you love.

STORIES OF INSPIRATION (LIKE OPRAH)

In 1978, Michal Jordan was just another sophomore trying out for the high school varsity basketball team. There were only fifteen spots. Do you think that Jordan, who would go on to score 32,292 points, earn six NBA championships, and win five NBA MVP titles, got one?

He did not make the team. But instead of quitting, he used his rejection as motivation. "Whenever I was working out and got tired and figured I ought to stop, I'd close my eyes and see that list in the locker room without my name on it," Jordan said. "That usually got me going again." The next year, he tried out for varsity again and made the team, becoming the best player on his high school team and averaging more than twenty points a game.

His failures did not end in high school. Jordan is famously quoted as saying, "I've missed more than 9,000 shots in my career. I've lost almost 300 games. Twenty-six times, I've been trusted to take the game-winning shot and missed. I've failed over and over and over again in my life. And that is why I succeed."

It's easy to see Michael Jordan's story as a unique—but it's not. Some of the most successful people in the world have endured significant setbacks—and have persevered through them to achieve their goals.

Want more proof?

- **Oprah Winfrey** was told by her first boss that she was "not right for television." She went on to host *The Oprah Winfrey Show*, one of the highest-ranking shows in history, and to become the richest self-made woman.

- **Steven Spielberg** was rejected from USC's prestigious film school not once, but three times. He has since won three Oscars and directed fifty-one iconic films, including *Jaws* and *Jurassic Park*.

- **Lady Gaga** was dropped by her first record label, Def Jam, in 2006 after only three months. Today, she is one of the best-selling musicians of all time.

- **Bill Gates**'s first entrepreneurial venture, Traf-O-Data, failed. He took the learnings and applied them to Microsoft, revolutionizing technology and becoming the youngest self-made billionaire at the age of 31.

- **Vera Wang** failed to make the US Olympic figure skating team after training for eleven years. Today, she is a major fashion designer, whose fashion empire is worth $1 billion.

- **Thomas Edison** was fired from his first two jobs and failed over 1,000 times in trying to create the lightbulb. In the end, he developed 1,093 patents and life-changing inventions, including the phonograph, the motion picture camera, and, of course, the electric light bulb.

Rejection is not unique to famous people. In my interviews for this book, I was surprised to learn how many times each person had experienced setbacks and the accompanying range of emotions, like disappointment, self-doubt, and frustration. These are people who have built remarkable careers—and they've all been rejected multiple times. Many have been laid off as well.

But they have one thing in common: they all kept going. Here are just a few of their stories.

Noah

During his senior year in college, Noah applied to twenty-two jobs—and received just one offer, not a top choice. Initially, Noah was devastated and wondered if he wasn't right the jobs he wanted. Upon reflection a few days later, he realized that he wasn't as sharp as he needed to be in his interviews. So, he developed a rigorous interview preparation approach that he used to get a job at a highly competitive private equity firm a few years later.

Pilar

After graduating from college, Pilar joined a top consulting company. Just a year later, she was laid off when the company downsized their workforce. While it was hard at the time, she's now grateful for what she learned from the experience. She said that it made her more open-minded about leaving jobs and looking for new opportunities. Seven years later, she had the courage to leave a prestigious company to found her own startup.

Stella

After a decade in healthcare, Stella decided that she wanted to work in technology. So, she updated her resume and submitted it online to ten companies—and heard nothing back.

Instead of giving up, Stella proactively sought feedback and learned that she needed to highlight her transferrable skills on her resume and network her way into jobs, versus dropping resumes online. By adjusting her approach, she landed a job at one of the most competitive technology firms in Silicon Valley—and she loves it.

I have known each of these people for years but never knew these stories. Rejection requires vulnerability to discuss, so people don't often talk about it. I am grateful to those who shared their experiences—because it makes us all realize that we aren't alone. So, share with your friends—and try to support them, too.

And when setbacks happen, remember: you're learning—and there is something amazing out there for you.

THE SECRET TO RESILIENCE: A GROWTH MINDSET

"Did I win? Did I lose? Those are the wrong questions. The correct question is: Did I make my best effort?"
—John Wooden, UCLA basketball coach
with the most NCAA national championships

People often think that skills like networking, interviewing, and negotiating are innate, but this perspective couldn't be further from the truth.

Just like learning anything in life, from how to make homemade bagels (I burned them the first time) to training for a marathon, job search skills are learned—and require lots of practice to become proficient. Your first networking calls may be a bit awkward. You may sound overly rehearsed in your first interviews. And there may be some long pauses in your first negotiations.

So how do you keep going when these things happen—or when you are feeling frustrated or discouraged? One simple mental shift: adopt a growth mindset. Stanford psychologist Carol Dweck pioneered the concept of a growth mindset—and it's life-changing. (If I could recommend only one book, it would be *Mindset*.)

With a growth mindset, you view a setback as a learning experience.

The beauty of a growth mindset is that anyone can adopt it at any time. You don't have to buy anything or spend years learning the concept. It's simply a choice—and something you can start doing right now.

So how do you adopt a growth mindset? Pay attention to your thoughts—then, reframe them. Let's say you just had an interview where you messed up the case question. Instead of telling yourself, "I'm awful at case interviews," ask yourself: *what did I learn?* Then, reframe your thought into a growth-oriented thought like "I'm still learning how to do case interviews, and this experience taught me what kinds of questions I need to study more before my next interview." Then, figure out what you still need to learn—and apply these things in your next interviews. As Professor Dweck says:

> *Think of times other people outdid you and you just assumed they were smarter or more talented. Now consider the idea that they just used better strategies, taught themselves more, practiced harder, and worked their way through obstacles. You can do that, too, if you want to.*

Even with a growth mindset, you will likely still experience the emotions that often accompany rejection, like frustration, disappointment, and sadness. Recent studies reveal that the same areas of the brain become activated when we experience rejection as when we experience physical pain. So, your reaction? It's biological. When this happens, acknowledge your feelings—and don't push yourself. Instead of applying for more jobs that day, do something that makes you happy, like going on a run, going out to eat or spending time with a friend.

Sometimes, disappointment can last for weeks—or even months. But you can still find a job you love, regardless of how you feel. You can feel scared and still send a networking email. You can feel nervous and still do well in an interview. You don't always need confidence to succeed. As Carol Dweck says:

> *A remarkable thing I've learned from my research is that in the growth mindset, you don't always need confidence . . . even when you think you're not good at something, you can still plunge into it wholeheartedly and stick to it.*

Adopting a growth mindset is life-changing. It can help you develop perseverance and the ability to stick with things that are hard—in the job search and beyond.

One more *very* important thing: prioritize the things you love in life during your search. Since job searching can be extremely stressful, making time to do the things you love is critical. Giving yourself time to enjoy life helps bring perspective, balance, and joy. And in the end, these things can give you the give you the resilience and motivation that leads to a more productive, and motivated, search.

Ask yourself the following question, and write down your answers.

LIFE PRIORITIES

What are your three favorite things to do in life?
1.
2.
3.

These things could include hanging out with your significant other, running, yoga, hiking, travelling the world, spending time with your kids, or anything else you really like.

Whatever you do, prioritize the things that bring you joy. Block time on your calendar if you need to—and then, do these things regularly.

And, remember:

Your life is so much more than your job.

---

7 SURPRISING REASONS WHY YOU MIGHT NOT GET THE JOB

I remember chatting with a friend who had just interviewed a candidate he really liked. They had a great conversation and bonded over their shared love of collecting vintage records, especially Led Zeppelin and Neil Young.

"So, you hired him, right?" I asked.

"Sadly, no," he replied.

They needed someone to manage a team of forty people, and he only had experience managing small teams. While he really liked the candidate, he didn't have the right experience. Sometimes your skills aren't right for the role or it's not a cultural match.

And, sometimes you don't get the job for reasons that have absolutely *nothing* to do with you. Here are seven common reasons:

SEVEN REASONS YOU MAY NOT GET THE JOB
(That have *nothing* to do with you)

1. There is no job.
This can happen during hiring freezes or when a team is only considering internal candidates, but the company requires the job to be posted externally.

2. The job disappears—or changes—during the process.

If sales drop 40 percent in a month, you probably won't get the job—because it won't exist anymore. Reorganizations can also cause positions to disappear. Sometimes during the recruiting process, the team redefines the role. Suddenly, they are looking for very different types of candidates from what they originally sought.

3. They never got your resume.

After posting a job description for a role on my team on our company website, I never saw 70 percent of the resumes submitted. Why? The antiquated online resume system required me to download each of the 172 resumes one-by-one. I didn't have time to do this, so I never saw the resumes for most people who applied. This is one of the reasons that it's ideal to apply for a job through someone at the company—see Chapter 6.

4. They forgot about you, even though they loved you.

After a first-round interview, Susan said that she would follow up with me at the end of the week. Three weeks later, I still hadn't heard from her. So, I sent her an email. Turns out, she was busy and had simply forgotten to reach out. She immediately set up a second-round interview—and I was eventually offered the job. People are busy, and this can happen. So, if you don't hear back, don't assume anything. Just follow up after a week or so. See below for example emails.

5. You were the top candidate—until the CEO's son applied.

You may have been the top candidate—until the CEO's son applied. Or a celebrity's daughter. It happens sometimes.

6. Your interviewer was having a bad day.

Sometimes, the person on the other end of the table is just having a bad day. Maybe their son threw a temper-tantrum on the way to school. Or maybe they spilled their coffee as they were walking out the door. We've all had those days.

7. You were overqualified.

I had a friend who graduated from college with a job private equity that would start in the fall. Until then, he was a broke college student who needed some extra cash for the summer. So, he applied at his favorite local deli. And his application? Denied. The manager said he was overqualified. This can happen. People are afraid that you will leave too soon, will get bored—or that they won't be able to pay you enough.

These scenarios all illustrate an important point. When you get rejected, don't assume anything. Instead, try the approaches below.

WHAT TO DO (SPECIFICALLY) WHEN YOU FACE SETBACKS

During her junior year in college in California, Mila applied for an internship at a startup in Austin that she *really* wanted. She didn't get the job and was surprised by the feedback: they were concerned that she didn't have any Texas connections and might be a retention risk. After giving her the news, they ended the conversation by saying, "But please keep in touch."

Instead of viewing her rejection as a closed door, Mila saw an opportunity and stayed in touch before reapplying the next year. She was offered the job.

Stay in touch with people *after* they reject you? This seems crazy—or does it?

As Mila's story illustrates, a rejection does not always equal a closed door. If you felt good about the interactions and would want to work there in the future, then stay in touch. (If the interview didn't go well, ask for feedback, and move on.)

Below are three common scenarios—and ideas for approaching each.

1. What do you do when you don't hear back after submitting your resume?

Your next steps depend on how you submitted your resume. If you sent it directly to a person at the company, follow up with a short email to that person.

EXAMPLE EMAIL
(*Situation*: You don't hear back after submitting your resume)

Hi Erin,

Thank you for offering to send my resume to Jennifer Tsang for her Finance Manager position a few weeks ago. I just wanted to follow up to see if you knew if there are any updates on the role?

Thanks again,
Lilia

If you submitted your resume online, try to find a contact for the job, which is often listed on the job description. Follow up with this person in a polite email inquiry, like the one above.

2. What do you do when you interview and don't hear back?

If you don't hear back after a week, follow up via email with the person who scheduled the interview (often an HR member), and inquire about next steps. Ideally, reply to the original email thread so they have context for who you are and the position for which you interviewed.

If you do not receive a response in a few days, you can follow up with a phone call.

A short simple email is best – here's an example:

EXAMPLE EMAIL
(*Situation*: You don't hear back after interviewing)

Hi Susan,

I really enjoyed meeting the team a couple weeks ago – thanks again for giving me the opportunity to interview for the Strategy Manager position. I just wanted to follow up to see if you have any updates?

Thank you,
Heather

3. What do you do when you don't get the job?

While a rejection is never pleasant, it can also be a great opportunity to learn how you can improve. When you hear "no," thank the company for giving you the opportunity to interview. Then, ask for feedback.

If you still want to work at the company and established a good rapport with your interviewers, ask if there are other jobs available that match your qualifications. You could say something like, "I love what you're doing at [the company]. Are you aware of any other open positions that might align with my experience?" Perhaps you would be a great match for another role that is open now—or sometime in the future.

If you think you would want to reapply in the future, keep in touch like Mila did. You never know what could happen.

WHEN THE UNIVERSE IS LOOKING OUT FOR YOU

Two weeks before graduation from her MBA program, Aria got some unexpected news: she no longer had a job. The company where she was planning to work rescinded all offers due to financial problems. Almost immediately, she let people know she was looking for a job and what types of roles she was seeking.

A few months later, an acquaintance came to her with an opportunity: to be a founding team member at a technology startup that she loved. This person introduced Aria to the CEO, who was impressed by her passion for the company and her business knowledge.

She got the job—and nine months later, the company was acquired for over $500 million. Aria was the fifth employee.

Sometimes, the universe is looking out for you—and saving you for something amazing in the future.

4. THE RESUME

THE BEST RESUME

How long do people spend, on average, reviewing your resume?

- 6 seconds
- 23 seconds
- 1 minute
- 3 minutes

Answer: *Six seconds!* That's all it takes to determine whether you get an interview. So, it's critical to create a resume that will pass this six second test.

The most important thing your resume must do is show that you are a *match* for the <u>specific</u> job.

And there's a highly-effective way to do this: the Six-Second Summary, which we will discuss later in the chapter. Your resume must also do a few other things.

When I talked to hiring managers at top companies, I asked them: "What does an amazing resume look like?" Here's what they said they look for:

- **Match for the Job.** Do you have the relevant skills and experiences for the position?

- **Communication Skills.** Is your resume clear, concise, and professional? Does it tell your professional and educational story clearly?

- **High Quality.** Is your resume well formatted and organized clearly? Is it grammatically correct and typo-free?

Your resume doesn't have to be perfect. Maybe you have a few resume blemishes: a low GPA (leave it off), a job that didn't last more than a year (use years for employment period), a time when you weren't working (explain with a cover letter).

Your resume is the most important tool for getting an interview—along with how you apply, which we will discuss in Chapter 6. So, grab your resume and sit down with some coffee—and prepare to create a resume that can lead to more interviews.

One thing to consider: as the world becomes more technology based, some recruiters will only want to see your LinkedIn profile. Ensure that you understand what the hiring manager wants you to send before you submit. Do they want your resume? Your LinkedIn profile? A cover letter? Or some combination of the three?

THE BEST RESUME DESIGN

After flipping through a stack of a hundred resumes, one stood out. In the top right-hand corner, there was a giant clip-art elephant. The applicant's school mascot?

To this day, I don't remember anything about the candidate's qualifications. He could have interned at NASA, founded a sanctuary for baby pandas, or had a 4.0 GPA. But I do remember deciding not to interview him because of the giant elephant on his resume.

There is lots of questionable resume advice out there. Most Google-generated sample resumes advise you to make your resume stand out with large, colored fonts or blocky layouts—but a resume is not the place to get creative. If you want to get artistic, buy some paints, grab an apron and some paintbrushes, and get in touch with your inner Jackson Pollack. Avoid these common resume pitfalls:

- Do not include photos, graphics, or images.
- Do not use colored text or paper.
- Do not use unique fonts.
- Do not use blocky layouts.

Your resume should stand out simply because of your qualifications—and nothing else.

RULE #1:
ONE PAGE ONLY

Have you ever been sitting in an interview and noticed that before the interviewer speaks, they are silently staring at your resume? That's probably because they didn't read it beforehand. Sometimes, that six-second review happens for the first time during the interview.

So, a short resume is best. Keep your resume to one page.

A one-page resume shows people why you are a *match* for the job—in only six seconds.

Don't worry about making your resume one page in your initial drafts. Condensing your resume to one page will be an exercise for the end. Once you've put all the content into your resume, go back and edit it. Make the content tighter and more concise until you reach the goal: one page.

The only exception to this rule is if you've been working for many years—generally fifteen or more. Even then, aim for one page if you can.

RULE #2:
USE FORMATTING BEST PRACTICES

To ensure that your resume gives the best first impression of you, use this *exact* Resume Template. All you need to do is enter your information into this document, using the guidelines in the rest of this chapter. Before you start, check out this great Sample Resume, which is organized, easy to read—and just one page. It's also included at the end of this chapter.

Follow these formatting conventions:

- **Font:** Arial or Times New Roman.

- **Font Size:** No larger than 12 point, except for your name at the top.

- **Sections:** Include only four sections: Summary, Professional Experience, Education, Additional.

- **Experiences:** List your jobs and educational experiences in descending order (i.e. most recent at the top).

- **Paper:** Use standard size paper, and PDF before you send via email.

Note: The template and recommendations below are for business roles in the United States. If you are applying in other countries or different fields, like graphic design, academia, or law, check for industry best practices and develop your resume according to these conventions.

TELLING YOUR (AWESOME) STORY

Often, when people create their resume, they include everything—every job, college activity, volunteer experience, skill, language, and work project. These resumes are often several pages long and read like an autobiography.

With this much detail, people usually cannot determine that you are the right match for the job in *only six seconds*. Instead, tell a story on your resume—the one that shows that you are a match for the jobs you are targeting.

The key to telling your story is identifying what is relevant and should be included (and excluded). Start by asking yourself the following questions.

QUESTIONS TO ASK YOURSELF
(Telling Your Story on Your Resume)

- What industries are you targeting?
- What functions are you targeting (e.g., sales, marketing, strategy)?
- Which of your experiences are relevant for jobs in these industries and functions?
  o Professional?
  o Educational?
  o Volunteer?
  o Other skills and interests?

As you start to think about how to tell this story, consider the following specific recommendations for what to include and exclude in each section of your resume.

PROFESSIONAL EXPERIENCES

Include	Exclude
• Full-time jobs and dates held • More detail under most recent jobs, specifically 3-5 bullet points for two most recent jobs and 1-2 bullet points for all other jobs	• Every project—only include the most relevant/ impactful • Irrelevant internships, especially if you are 3+ years out of college

EDUCATION

Include	Exclude
• All degrees and years achieved • GPA—only if 3.0 or higher • Test Scores—only if high • Academic Honors (Cum Laude, Phi Beta Kappa, etc.) • Scholarships • Student organizations that are 1) relevant to the job, 2) where you held a leadership position, or 3) that are otherwise notable	• Student organizations that are 1) irrelevant, 2) that you don't want affiliated with your identity (e.g., Thursday Night Drinking Club), or 3) where you were not a leader, especially if you are more than three years out of college

ADDITIONAL

Include	Exclude
• Appropriate interests (e.g. hiking, running, painting) • Relevant skills (languages, certifications, proficiency in unique programs for industry)	• Too many/ inappropriate interests • Irrelevant skills • Too much volunteer work

• Volunteer work – curated and/ or relevant	

Write down each job you've held, in descending order with the most recent at the top of your resume. Do the same for your educational experiences and additional section. Based on these guidelines, jot down what you want to include under each.

This will be helpful for the next step: creating great bullet points for each experience.

HOW TO CRAFT AMAZING BULLET POINTS

Have you ever seen a bullet point on a resume that says something like "Optimized ARTs to generate 54% increase in PST"?

And you wonder, what does that *mean*? It's probably impressive, but it might as well be in another language. I don't know if ARTs are real or if PWT stands for anything—and that's the point. There are industry words or company-specific terms that might as well be fictitious—because people outside of your company or industry will have no idea what they mean.

You must *translate* your experiences on your resume.

As you're working through drafts, get feedback. Send your resume to a friend, ideally a person outside of your company and industry. Ask them if your resume makes sense. Do they understand what you did?

Use these guidelines to create effective bullet points:

- **Translate your experiences.** Ensure that people outside your company/industry would understand what you did. Exclude company-specific vocabulary and industry-specific language, if you are switching industries.

- **Use action verbs.** Start your bullet points with strong action verbs to convey what *you* specifically did. Use words like "developed," "optimized," "launched," "managed," etc. Avoid words like "helped," as it's assumed that you were a member of a team.

- **Show impact—and be specific.** Show the *specific* impact of your work. This is critical, as hiring managers are looking for candidates who understand how their work impacted the bigger organization. For example, instead of saying "Worked with hotel to improve profits," say "Increased hotel profits by 35% through targeted digital marketing campaign." The first bullet point is vague, and the impact is unclear. The second one is impressive.

- **Be concise.** Use only one line per bullet point—two maximum. A bullet point that is more than two lines is usually confusing and often a run-on sentence.

- **Include more detail on more recent/relevant roles.** Include 3-5 bullet points for your most recent and relevant positions. For all other roles, include only 1-2 bullet points.

Start developing your bullet points. An amazing resume is not created in just one draft. You will likely go through several drafts as you craft your story. Write your bullet points now—and then put your resume away to be reviewed again in a day or two.

HOW TO TELL THE STORY OF THE PERSON BEHIND THE PAPER

Add an "Additional" section at the bottom of your resume, and include things like volunteer experience, skills, and interests. Shared interests can help build rapport during an interview. It's always great to hear your interviewer say something like "Oh, you like backpacking, too?" What a great way to build a connection.

One note here is to use discretion in the interests you include. Things like rock climbing, hiking, and espresso tasting are great. Things like collecting antique tweezers, self-tattooing, and nude-beach volleyball may raise some eyebrows.

Include volunteer work, relevant skills, or language skills in this section as well. One word of caution: make sure you state your actual skill level. The story below provides a good lesson.

If you majored in Spanish, it seems reasonable to write "fluent in Spanish" on your resume, right? This is what a good friend did in college. Then, he submitted his resume to an investment bank in New York. Imagine his surprise when he walked into his first interview, and the interviewer said, "Hola!" And then proceeded to conduct the *entire interview* in Spanish.

Luckily, he could speak enough Spanish to get through the interview. But it made him realize that he wasn't fluent in a native-speaker-kind-of-way. So, he changed "fluent" to "proficient"—and never had to do another interview in Spanish.

Often people forget to include impressive accomplishments outside of their specific work projects. In six seconds, a reviewer probably won't connect the dots to figure out that you were promoted two times in three years, managed five people, were identified as a top ten percent performer, and led the Women's Initiative.

Make sure you explicitly call out things like:

- Being promoted
- Managing people
- Being selected for special leadership programs
- Leading committees
- Special projects

These are important parts of your work experience—so state them explicitly, using a separate bullet point for each.

THE SECRET TO GETTING MORE INTERVIEWS

Have you ever not applied for a job because you didn't have all the qualifications listed on the job description? Studies have shown that this is more common for women. Men apply for a job when they meet only 60 percent of the qualifications, but women often apply only if they meet 100 percent of them. But often job descriptions are written more as a wish list than as a set of definitive requirements.

You can, and should, apply to jobs you want, even when you don't have all the qualifications. And there's one small thing to add to your resume that will help get an interview, even without all the qualifications: the Six-Second Summary.

First, let's talk about what the Six-Second Summary is not. It is **not** a list of all the ambiguous business skills that people think they need. For example:

Networking skills, detail-orientation, team-building, communication, change management, analytical skills . . . *this is generic, no one is good at all these things, are you still reading this?*

With the Six Second Summary, you highlight the *specific* experiences that make you well qualified for *each* job for which you apply—based on the job description.

Let's talk through an example. Say that Everly Miller (our resume example) is applying for a Director of Digital Strategy role. These are the qualifications on the job description:

- Strategy experience, including 3-5 years of management consulting
- An innovative mindset and approach

- Experience managing large teams

So, Everly asks herself: *What skills and experience qualify me for this specific job?* Then, she highlights these in her Six-Second Summary at the top of her resume, using words from the job description:

SUMMARY

Professional with Tuck MBA and consulting experience at Accenture; strengths include:

- **Strategic expertise,** including development of go-to-market strategy for a bestselling almond milk
- **Creativity and innovation,** including developing new products at Arrow + Modern based on research to understand the customer of the future
- **Managing teams,** achieving a top 10% rating of managers at Accenture

---

The Six-Second Summary is effective because it highlights your *relevant* experience for the *specific* role. And it's easy to read in six seconds. (Seriously, try it.)

As you write your own Six-Second Summaries, try to follow these three general rules.

SIX SECOND SUMMARY RULES

1. Be concise.
Follow the provided format. Use a bold headline and include three bullet points underneath that are ideally one line, two lines max.

2. Highlight your relevant experiences.
Read each job description carefully, and use your Six-Second Summary to highlight your top three relevant skills and experiences for *each* job. Use the exact words from the job description, like Everly did with "strategic expertise," "innovation," and "managing teams." (This means that your Six-Second Summary will be different for each position for which you apply.)

3. Use specific examples.
Use specific examples, ideally the most impressive for each skill, such as when you increased sales by 20 percent, organized thirty

speakers at a conference, or launched a new product.

There are usually many qualifications on a job description, so people often ask: *how do you determine which qualifications ones are most important for the job?* Think about the role and read the job description closely to see if something is mentioned multiple times.

When you lack certain qualifications, highlight the relevant experience you *do* have. When companies find candidates they love that lack some of the qualifications, they sometimes hire them anyways. Why? Often because:

People hire people they like.

A NOTE ON RESUME VERSIONING

You will have several different versions of your resume, one for each role for which you apply and a general version. Start by creating the general version—the one you will send to people when there is not a specific job (e.g. when networking). For the Six Second Summary on your general version, highlight the three strengths that you hope to use in your next job

Since you will be customizing the Six Second Summary for each job for which you apply, you will end up with several company-specific versions of your resume. To save these, create separate folders by company, and save your resume using your name and date (e.g. "Smith_Seren.2018.04.17").

Finally, PDF your resume before you send it electronically.

PROOFREAD, PROOFREAD, PROOFREAD

When reviewing candidates for an open role, a friend came upon a resume whose creator had a unique skill: "managing steakholders." But this was for a job in healthcare, not on a ranch. Proofread. Proofread. Proofread.

Specifically, look for:

- Typos
- Grammatical errors (e.g., its vs. it's, affect vs. effect, ensure vs. insure)
- Formatting errors (e.g., different fonts, incorrect punctuation)

If grammar is not your strong suit, ask for proofreading help from a friend who writes well.

Additionally, try to get feedback from someone who does not work at your company—or in your industry if you plan to switch industries. This person should have no idea what you do at work each day.

When they review your resume, ask them the following questions:

1. Does my resume make sense?
2. Do you understand what I do in my current job? In past roles?
3. Is there too much or too little detail?
4. Is there any vocabulary that does not make sense to you?
5. Are there any typos or grammatical errors?
6. Any other recommendations that you have?

Then, incorporate their feedback if you think it makes sense, and *always* proofread one last time before you send your resume. (And PDF before you send.)

HOW TO CREATE A STAND-OUT LINKEDIN PROFILE

According to a recent survey, 94 percent of recruiters use LinkedIn to source and vet candidates, while only 36 percent of people looking to change positions are active on the site.

LinkedIn is becoming increasingly important in the job search.

Here are common ways people who could hire you will use it:

- **Recruiters and headhunters** search for candidates
- **Interviewers** look at candidate profiles
- **People you network with** look you up beforehand

So, after creating your resume, the next thing to do is to develop your LinkedIn profile, or update it if you already have one. As a technology company, LinkedIn is constantly making improvements and upgrading their platform. So, it can be worthwhile to read a few recent articles before you start working on your profile. Even so, there are some basic rules to follow in creating your profile, which are below.

Before you start, know this: LinkedIn is not the same as your resume. What does this mean? At a high level, LinkedIn should include the same experiences on your resume: the same jobs, educational experiences and volunteer experiences. Instead of bullet points, include a couple sentences under each experience that are concise and easy to understand—even for someone outside of your industry.

Here are some specific tips on how to approach each section of your profile:

HOW TO CREATE YOUR LINKEDIN PROFILE

Headline

LinkedIn automatically populates your headline with your current job title and company, but you can change it. If you want people to find your profile through search, try to include important keywords. For example, if you are seeking jobs in supply chain, you could include the word "Operations" in your headline. Try to keep your headline short—about ten words, maximum. And avoid using slashes between critical keywords, for example, "operations/sales," as the LinkedIn search technology does not always recognize it.

Instead use a vertical slash with spaces, like "Operations | Sales."

Summary

Think about what you think you want. Do you want a job in a certain industry? Are you targeting a certain type of role? Include keywords (e.g. marketing, sales, operations, strategy, etc.) in your summary since they will help you show up in searches done by recruiters. Your summary should also include relevant experience and align with others in your target industry. Look at peoples' summaries who work in the jobs you want. What do they have in common? Are they short? Are they long? Are they more casual? More formal? Do they tell stories? Or do they simply summarize their experience? Look at several peoples' summaries and try to figure out what you think works best in the industry you are targeting – and then, create your own based on your research.

Professional History

Include your past roles, including company, title and the dates that you held each position. If you have had multiple roles at the same company, ensure that these are easily visible on your LinkedIn profile to show your diversity of experience and any promotions. If any of your job titles are company specific, you may want to consider changing the wording to make them more easily understandable.

Description of Each Role

Great profiles include two to three concise, clear sentences on what you did in each role.

Educational History

Include all degrees, both undergraduate and graduate, and any honors or activities. Try to curate these – and choose your top three activities and honors from each educational experience.

Photo

Include a photo that is recent, professional and looks the part for the job you want. What does this mean? A picture where you look like you—but not like you're at a music festival and cropped out your friend. You don't have to spend money on your photo. If you don't have a good picture, ask a friend to take one of you against a white wall or neutral background—and make sure the lighting is good. You don't have to be wearing a suit—it's fine to just wear a solid top. If you're targeting more casual companies and roles, a grey t-shirt could be fine. LinkedIn now enables you to apply filters to your photo. Black and white is always a good choice.

Fill out as much of your profile as possible – there is a meter at the top that measures the completion level of your profile. The more complete it is, the more often it shows up in search results—which can mean more job opportunities.

NEXT LEVEL LINKEDIN

Here are some additional features that can make your search experience with LinkedIn even better. If you are interested in any of these, you can find instructions on how to implement each using Google.

1. **Customize your URL:** You can customize your LinkedIn URL. The default will be something like: https://www.linkedin.com/in/heather-hund-3114a2a/ but you can customize it to be cleaner: https://www.linkedin.com/in/heather-hund.

2. **Be anonymous:** People can see if you have viewed their profiles. If you want to turn this feature off (e.g. show up as 'Anonymous' if you view someone's profile), you can change this in your privacy controls.

3. **Use the Open Candidates feature:** This feature enables you to indicate which types of jobs you are looking for, and

this information is available to recruiters (but not generally publicly available).

ON COVER LETTERS

There are a lot of opinions out there on cover letters. Here's mine: skip it—with a few caveats. Only write a cover letter if 1) it's required, or 2) you feel that you need to explain something, like a long time out of the workforce. Other people feel differently. Some think you should always write a cover letter. And some companies strongly consider cover letters. Others don't.

In my experience, cover letters often serve to filter out candidates, not to strengthen their application. A cover letter is an exhibition of your writing skills, which can damage your candidacy if you are not an excellent writer. And writing might not even be important for the job.

Email seems to be taking the place of cover letters these days. Instead of the cover letter, I strongly recommend focusing on the email you write asking someone to send your resume to the hiring manager, as discussed in Chapter 6.

If you write a cover letter, convey your interest in the role and company. Then, explain why you are good fit for the job, using specific examples from your resume. Highlight the skills that you used in your Six-Second Summary. And ensure that your cover letter is typo-free, grammatically correct, and well structured.

See the last page of the chapter for a cover letter example that follows these conventions.

EVERLY L. MILLER*

Seattle, WA • Phone Number • Email • LinkedIn Link

SUMMARY

Professional with Tuck MBA and consulting experience at Accenture; strengths include:
- Strategic expertise, including development of go-to-market strategy for a bestselling almond milk
- Creativity and innovation, including developing new products at Arrow + Modern based on research to understand the customer of the future
- Managing teams, achieving a top 10% rating of managers at Accenture

PROFESSIONAL EXPERIENCE

Modern + Arrow	Ventura, CA
Product Operations – Director	2014-Present

- Lead pre-season product testing for this modern clothing company, both in store and online
- Developed digital product testing, growing the program to test 20% of all online products in 9 months, resulting in a revenue increase of 15%
- Manage team of nine – ranked in top 10% of managers
- Promoted twice after only eleven months in each role; selected for high performance leadership program
- Work cross-functionally with leaders across brands to drive testing integration; functions included Merchandising, Inventory Management, Marketing, Store Operations, and CEM

Digital Strategy – Sr. Manager 2013-2104
- Supported Will Parker, Digital Vice President, to grow online business and drive digital innovation
- Led pilot of online product testing initiative across six brands, leading to company adoption
- Developed e-commerce strategy that resulted in online sales growth of 20% in a year

Accenture	Denver, CO
Consultant	2012-2013

- Developed a transformation strategy for a retailer by conducting market, competitor, and consumer insight analyses to determine the optimal omni-channel approach to enhance profitability
- Optimized sales at a consumer company through a customer data analysis to inform sales team reorganization
- Developed and implemented a culture change strategy at a Fortune 500 company during a reorganization; led multiple workshops with the leadership team to foster behavioral change

JP Morgan	Dallas, TX
Associate – Real Estate Private Equity Group	2005-2009

- Managed +$1 billion of assets, with a focus on hotels and office properties
- Built financial models to value assets and to determine asset strategies (i.e., renovations, sales) based on ROI
- Wrote bi-annual investor reports and other investor communications for six funds

EDUCATION

Dartmouth College – Tuck School of Business	Hanover, NH
MBA	2009-2011

- President – Retail Club, Women in Management, Pro-Bono Consulting Team

University of Arizona	Tucson, AZ
BBA Finance, Minor in Spanish (GPA 3.6/4.0)	2001-2005

- Dean's Scholarship (100 selected from 1,500), Top Finance Major Award, Phi Beta Kappa

ADDITIONAL

Interests: Writing, rock climbing, half-marathons, snow skiing, hiking, travel

This resume is fictional and created for illustrative purposes only.

Modern + Arrow
Melissa Arbuckle
San Francisco, California
Re: Manager – Finance and Planning

April 17, 2018

Dear Melissa,

I am writing to express my interest in the Strategy Manager position at Modern + Arrow. I have been a loyal customer of Modern + Arrow since it launched in 2015 and an advocate for the brand. I love your modern designs and am inspired by your mission to introduce sustainability into the world of home design.

At Modern + Arrow, I would leverage over a decade of experience in strategy and retail, including:

- **E-commerce experience,** including developing an e-commerce strategy for an apparel retailer that generated 20% in top line growth

- **Strategy consulting** at Accenture, where I worked with ten Fortune 500 companies, including three major omni-channel retailers

- **Managing teams** at Accenture, where I was ranked in the top 10% of managers

- **Working with executives**, including 30+ senior leaders at ten Fortune 500 companies

I would be thrilled to support your team in its next phase of growth. Thank you for the consideration, and I look forward to hearing from you.

Sincerely,

Emily Grovesbeck
Emily.grovesbeck@abcd.com
(454)-200-2001

5. NETWORKING

PEOPLE REALLY WANT TO HELP YOU

When I left a past role, I was reluctant to tell others since I didn't have another job lined up and hadn't started looking. A couple of weeks later, my husband and I were having dinner with friends when one asked me about my job. I paused before sharing that I had quit and was searching for another job.

To my surprise, he exclaimed, "*Congratulations!*" Then, he offered to help. That week, we had a phone call to discuss my interests. He connected me to several people in his network and sent me great industry newsletters and resources. He was so kind and helpful—and I was so glad I had shared that I was searching with him.

Often, when we embark on a search, we are terrified to tell anyone. And this puts us at a significant disadvantage—because the best way to find jobs is through other people. According to research, 85 percent of jobs are acquired through networking. What if your best friend were looking for a new job? Or an acquaintance you barely knew? Would you want to help them? Most people will want to help you as well. In studies at Stanford University, researchers found that people drastically underestimated the number of strangers on the street who would help them—by up to 50 percent.

People want to help you—so much more than you think.

Asking for help can also build deeper relationships. When someone asks you for help, it usually requires some vulnerability. And as Brené Brown discusses in her TED Talk, being vulnerable makes people closer and, in turn, makes our lives richer and more meaningful. As she says, "Connection is why we're here. It's what gives purpose and meaning to our lives."

So, tell people that you are looking for a job, starting with family and friends. Tell them what you are interested in. If they can help, they probably will.

NETWORKING CAN BE (AT LEAST KIND OF) FUN

Networking has a bad reputation. Before I understood what it was, I thought that networking involved wearing a sticky nametag and wandering around stuffy hotel conference rooms trying to break into impenetrable conversation circles. Networking seemed unpleasant and awkward—and I *never* wanted to network like that. You don't have to do that either.

What I have found is that the most effective, and most enjoyable, way to network is simply to talk to people one-on-one in person or over the phone. Here are the basics:

NETWORKING BASICS

- **Be strategic in how you approach networking.** Make a list of people you want to contact using the Networking

<u>Tracker</u>. Start by educating yourself on the industry and then follow the approach in the 'How to Start Networking' section. As discussed below, start with friends and family since they can help you become more educated and better prepared for your future conversations.

- **Send an email—if you know the person.** Networking requests are usually best initiated by sending an email and asking someone to chat, ideally in person but on the phone works too. More on how to write networking emails is below.

- **Ask for a connection—if you don't know the person.** If you want to connect with someone you don't know, ask a mutual connection to introduce you. This type of intro is often called a warm intro—because while you don't know the person, you aren't reaching out cold. How do you discover these connections? LinkedIn. If you share several mutual connections, be strategic about who you ask to introduce you. The stronger the connection, the more likely the response.

- **Reach out a couple of weeks before you want to chat.** Usually it takes a couple weeks to get on someone's calendar. If they are more senior, it can take even longer, often up to a month.

- **Keep pursuing your goals—regardless of how people respond.** If someone hasn't responded after a couple weeks, follow up. Even then, know that not everyone will respond, and don't let this discourage you from networking. Sometimes people won't respond – and some will say, "no." See if there's anything you can learn—and either way, don't give up. This is part of networking—and something that you will likely encounter on your path to finding a job you love.

So, why is it critical to network in your job search? Networking serves two main purposes:

1. Networking will help you find jobs.
Networking is like a web. In most cases, the person you talk to will not have a job available—but may connect you to others in the industry, ultimately leading to opportunities. Networking becomes even more critical as you become more senior—often these roles aren't posted online and are found exclusively through networking.

Even if the role you want is posted online, it's still critical to network. Why? Because on average, 120 people apply for each open role. If you apply through someone at the company (e.g. someone that you meet through networking), you become a personal recommendation—which gives you a significant advantage over the other anonymous applicants.

2. Networking will help you figure out what you want to do.
Networking can help you answer the ultimate question: *What do you want to do?* Specifically, what companies do you want to work for? And what types of jobs sound interesting? Networking can help you explore and learn about roles, industries, and companies. You may also learn about interesting roles that you didn't even know existed.
Networking can help you answer questions like:

- What do people *really* do in their role?
- What is the culture of the company like?
- What do people like most and least about their job?
- What do career paths look like?
- What are the most influential areas of the company?
- How is the industry changing? How is it impacting the company?

Through these discussions, you can learn a lot about a company—from "Here are the groups that are doing the most interesting things," to "We're headed for major layoffs. . ."

In a prior search, I talked to over fifty people and found most of these conversations to be highly informative—and enjoyable. (A few were awkward, which happens on occasion.) Over time, my conversations became much less scripted and more casual. Networking also led to the development of a few solid, long-term relationships.

I recommend networking a lot—in a way that works for you. If you're working full time and not rushed to switch jobs, perhaps aim for two or three conversations per week. Or if you are job searching full time, you could aim for ten conversations per week.

That's not to say that you won't have an awkward interaction along the way. Sometimes, networking conversations are just awkward. You're usually talking to people you've never met and will likely encounter a range of personalities. When you have an awkward conversation, try to let it go—because you will have some truly amazing conversations as well.

HOW TO START NETWORKING

Make a list of *all* the companies you are interested in. Write them down in Column B of your Networking Template, which can be found on the *Art of the Job Search* website and can help you stay strategic and organized as you network.

What if you don't know what companies you are interested in? Or if your list is small? Your list will grow as you network, but you can also expand it now.

Here's how to discover interesting companies:

- **LinkedIn:** Go to the Companies page on LinkedIn, and type in a company name. On each company page, scroll down. On the lower right hand side, you will see a list of similar companies under a heading called, "People also viewed..."

- **Crunchbase:** Interested in working at a startup? Go to the Companies tab on the Crunchbase website, and add filters to find companies that match your criteria. For example, you could find a list of all the early-stage technology startups in Austin or all the healthcare startups in San Francisco.

- **Other people:** Tell people what you are looking to do, even if it's not specific. Start with your friends and family since they most want to help you. They might have ideas of companies to explore—and potentially even know people there and offer to connect you.

Once you've made your networking list, rank your list of companies using a very simple system: A, B, C.

NETWORKING: COMPANY RANKING SYSTEM

1. A = Best. You would *love* to work there.
2. B = Better. You would like to work there, but not as much as at your A companies.
3. C = Good. You would like to work there, but not as much as your A or B companies.

How do you prioritize where to network first? Begin networking with friends and family in your target industries and companies since you can ask them your basic questions to become more educated. Once you feel educated and clear on your story and what you want, reach out to people who work at your A companies, ideally starting with the people at companies you would most want to work—since networking can lead to job opportunities. (Note that this type of networking process can take time—several months. You can condense it by reaching out to more people at once.)

Before you reach out to anyone, Google yourself first. During a recent interview process, Chao found a candidate she really liked. Before making an offer, she Googled him—and found a website he created titled *Bitcoin Savage* featuring his bitmoji sitting on a bejeweled throne and throwing gold coins into the air. It was probably a joke, but she still couldn't hire him—just in case that hubris was real.

So, before you start networking, Google yourself. Why? Because a lot of people will be Googling you in the job search: people you network with, hiring managers, recruiters, interviewers, headhunters—and more.

When you Google yourself, what do you find? Are you happy with what you see? Or are there any questionable photos? Or websites? Or anything else that you would rather not be publicly available?

Check all your accounts: Facebook, Twitter, Instagram, etc. If there is anything questionable, remove it. How do you do it? Google for instructions on how to remove things from each site. You can remove pretty much anything—Facebook posts, pictures, or search results on Google.

Once you've cleaned up your web profile, it's time for the next step: finding people to network with.

FINDING THE +250,000 PEOPLE IN YOUR NETWORK

How many people are in your network? Probably over a quarter of a million.

The average person has 500 LinkedIn connections. If each of these 500 people is also connected to 500 people, that means that you are connected to 250,000 people.

Your network is likely larger than all but eighty-three cities in the United States. Within this network, there are three primary sources that will be useful in your search:

- Friends and family
- Friends of friends
- Alumni networks

THREE NETWORKING SOURCES

1. Friends and Family

Start here. Tell your friends and family you are looking for a job first. Why? Because they most want to help you, and if they work in your target industries or companies can often educate you by answering your more basic questions. Tell them you are job searching and share what you are interested in. Ask if there are any companies that seem interesting—and if they know anyone who works there.

2. Friends of Friends

A friend of a friend . . . is also a friend. LinkedIn is primarily how you will find them. These are your second-degree connections. Before you start, ensure that your LinkedIn profile is complete and prepared for your job search, as discussed in Chapter 4. Then, do the following:

1. **Update your connections.** Search LinkedIn for people you know and invite them to connect.

2. **Subscribe to LinkedIn Premium.** While paying a monthly fee can seem ridiculous in the age of free everything on the internet, this one is worth it, especially during the networking phase of your search. LinkedIn Premium enables you to view your connections' networks—and their detailed profiles.

3. **Set the anonymous setting (optional).** If you don't want other people to see that you have viewed their profile, set the anonymous setting on LinkedIn. Google for instructions.

Once you've done these things, use LinkedIn Premium to identify friends of friends that you want to network with. Then, ask your friends to introduce you. If you don't know the connector well, it can make sense to try to have coffee with them first. Do what feels appropriate in the situation given your relationship with the person.

Know that you are asking a favor, so be thoughtful about what you are asking from other people, especially if you aren't that close or if they are very senior or pressed for time. Also know that people will sometimes say "no." Perhaps they don't know the person well enough, or don't think the person has time to connect.

Here's an example email below asking for an introduction.

EXAMPLE EMAIL
(*Situation*: Asking a friend to make a networking connection)

Subject: Connect to James Wills?

Hi Jen,

Hope this note finds you well! I am currently looking for my next position and am seeking to find a role in the food industry with a sustainability angle.

I noticed on LinkedIn that you're connected with James Wills, who works at Fish + Ocean. I enjoyed his new take on sustainable ocean fishing in his recent article on Medium and would love to chat with him to learn more about his experience and perspectives on the industry. Any chance you might be able to connect us? No worries if you don't know him well or if it doesn't feel appropriate.

I've included a bit more information about my background below, which might be helpful for you to share with him if you are able to connect us.

All the best,
Jared

Bio

Jared has spent the past three years working in management consulting at Deloitte, primarily in consumer packaged goods. He is looking to transition into the organic food industry, where he aims to leverage his experience in strategy and his passion for organic food.

He is inspired by Fish + Ocean's sustainable fishing practices and is looking to learn more about the company. Prior to Deloitte, he attended the Wharton School of Business and received a BA from Grinnell in English.

3. Alumni Networks

What networks do you belong to? Undergrad networks? Grad school networks? Company alumni networks? Any other networks?

Search your networks to try to find people who work in industries or at companies that you are looking to learn more about. Then, reach out to them.

As mentioned above, sometimes people won't respond to your networking requests—and they may occasionally say no. But it's often a function of good intentions. They wanted to introduce you to their friend—and forgot, or they have three kids and are working on a really demanding project at work and didn't have time.

When people don't respond, reach out again after a couple weeks. And if people never respond or say "no," don't let this deter you from networking.

People have said "no" in my searches and many have not responded, but so many others have said "yes"—and have been incredibly nice and helpful. If I had stopped networking simply because someone said no or didn't respond, I would have missed out on some amazing conversations and opportunities.

Below is a sample networking email for someone in your alumni network.

EXAMPLE EMAIL

(*Situation*: Asking someone in an alumni network to chat)

Subject: Grinnell Alum chat?

Hi James,

Hope this note finds you well! I graduated from Grinnell in 2006 and recently decided to transition from management consulting into the organic food space. I saw on the Alumni network that you work at Common Food. I'm impressed by your work in the industry and loved your recent article on the best ways to brand and market organic food in *Modern Farming*.

Wondering if you might be free to chat in the next few weeks? Would love to get your perspective and advice.

All the best,
Jared

WHEN SHOULD YOU NETWORK?

A common misperception people have is that they need to wait to network until they have "figured things out." It depends what you are trying to figure out. If you're trying to learn more about the technology industry before you talk to the COO of a startup that you really want to work for, that is definitely the best approach. In that case, start with friends and lower-level people, so you can be more educated about the industry and company before talking to an executive. And then research the company extensively and build a list of questions, using the guidance below.

But if someone connects you to a friend of theirs, chat with them. Often, networking *is* figuring things out and can help build connections that can lead to jobs. (Still take the time to research the company and build a thoughtful list of questions).

Keep in mind as well that networking meetings can take a while to schedule. Usually, it takes at least a week or two to get on someone's calendar. Rarely will someone be free to chat the next day. However, if it's urgent, you can say something like "I have an interview with your company next Wednesday. Would love to ask you a few questions beforehand—any chance you might be able to chat before then?"

Networking is simply opening a door. If the conversation goes well, ask if they have any current openings that match what you are looking to do. Often, there won't be jobs available now—but there might in the future. If that happens, reach out to that person again to chat about a role of interest, or you can ask them to pass your resume to the hiring manager. (If you had a *really* strong connection, keep in touch—and perhaps try to meet with them again in a month or two.)

Some people will also say, "Let me know where you end up." Let them know what job you take, as this could lead to the development of a long-term relationship. Who knows what could happen in the future? Maybe you will work together someday.

A NETWORKING SCRIPT + QUESTIONS

Here's the secret to a great networking conversation: be prepared. After all, each conversation could lead to your next job. (But know that it will likely require tons of networking.) So, before your conversations:

- **Research the company beforehand.** Spend time on the company website. Google the company to find recent news. Check the careers page on the company website to see if there are any open roles that you are interested in. If it's a casual chat and your goal is to learn, then try to spend fifteen minutes researching the company. If it's with someone senior and you really want the job, prepare more extensively. (Chapter 7 discusses how to prepare for an interview – you can use a similar, and slightly less extensive, approach for networking.)

- **Be prepared to lead the conversation.** You asked for the meeting, so by default, you lead the conversation. What does this mean? Start by introducing yourself, and be prepared with the questions you want to ask. Most conversations are a two-way dialogue, but if the conversation stalls, it's up to you to fill the gap. See below for a script you can follow and questions you can ask.

- **Prepare questions in advance.** What do you want out of the conversation? Figure this out, and then develop questions accordingly. There is a list of questions below that can serve as a starting point for developing your own. If you are meeting in person, memorize them or write bullet points in your notebook, as the best networking conversations are often the more casual ones.

- **Look up the person on LinkedIn beforehand.** This can help you understand their background and enable you to connect over any experiences you share, like attending the same school or working at the same company.

If you aren't sure how to approach your networking conversations, see below for a detailed approach for conducting a conversation from start to finish. As you network more, you will find that these conversations will become more natural, and I encourage you to approach them in a way that's authentic to you.

As you're learning, you can follow the structure and approach outlined below.

NETWORKING: THE CONVERSATION (A SCRIPT)

I. Opening/Small Talk

Open the discussion by trying to make small talk. It helps to foster a connection that can make the conversation more comfortable—on both ends. You can start with something like "How's your day going?" or "How was your weekend?" Try to find a connection and chat briefly until it feels like the right time to dive into the discussion.

II. Introductions

Next, exchange introductions. Start by giving them context for why you are calling and a brief introduction about yourself. It might go something like this:

> *Thanks for taking the time to chat today. A little bit of background about why I reached out—I just left management consulting and am looking to transition into marketing. At Accenture, I primarily focused on strategy for technology companies. I really enjoyed marketing projects, including one where we redefined the social media strategy for an e-commerce company, so I am aiming to shift into a marketing role. I'm looking to learn more about your experience in marketing at Amazon and have some questions for you.*

Your intro should include three elements:

- What you seek to do
- A concise overview of your background
- An expression of gratitude

Ensure that your intro is clear and concise—no more than a minute. After you prepare your intro, practice it in the mirror and ideally with someone else.

After you give your intro, ask the person to share their background. Even if looked them up on LinkedIn beforehand, this gives them the chance to tell you their story and enables you to ask questions about their experiences.

III. Questions

Think about what information *you* want out of the conversation—and then, ask targeted questions to get it. The questions you ask will differ based on how well you know the person you are talking to and how senior they are. The questions below are categorized accordingly.

When speaking with senior people or when you know there's a job available that you want, prepare for your conversation more extensively, using the interview preparation techniques in Chapter 7. Prepare insightful questions that show knowledge about the company—and be ready to articulate the type of job you are looking for if asked.

Try to prepare at least ten questions and prioritize them, placing the most critical ones at the top of your list. In thirty minutes, you may not make it through many questions, especially if it turns into more of a dialogue. Also, you can take notes—and *should* if it's a call. These can be helpful to review if you get an interview at the company.

Below are some questions you could ask, categorized according to the level of the person you are talking to.

NETWORKING QUESTIONS

For same / more junior levels:

The questions below are a starting point—and best for exploratory conversations. Choose the ones that feel most relevant, and try to develop your own as well based on what you want out of the conversation.

- Can you tell me more about your background?
- Can you tell me about your experience at the company?
- Can you tell me more about what you do in your current position?
- What do you enjoy most about your position?
- What do you enjoy least about your position?

- What are the key focus initiatives in the company right now?
- What are the priorities this year?
- What are the major areas of growth in the company?
- What does the career path for someone in your position typically look like?
- Can you describe the culture of the company?
- How would you describe the work/life balance?
- How does the recruiting process work?
- Is there anything I can do or provide to be helpful to you?

If the conversation is going well and it feels appropriate, you can ask one or more of the following questions:

- I saw an open role online that I am interested in. Can you tell me more about this position?
- I am interested in [type of role]. I did not find any open roles online like this—are you aware of any?
- Is there anyone else you think I should talk to?
- Are there any other companies you would recommend I explore?

For more senior levels:
Ideally, prepare as if you were interviewing—see Chapter 7 for how to research the company and prepare appropriately. You can pull some of the questions from above, and I highly recommend creating custom questions of your own.

If you are talking to a friend, you can often ask very honest questions, like the potential salary range for the position, specific policies (e.g., tuition reimbursement, maternity leave, vacation days), their opinion of the hiring manager, thoughts on an open role, etc. Ask only the questions that feel appropriate based on your relationship and the conversation.

IV. Closing

Before you hang up, thank the person again. You can say something like this:

Thank you so much for taking the time to chat. I really appreciate you sharing your experiences and insight. You've had such an interesting career—and our conversation has been very helpful.

V. Follow-Up

Always follow up with a thank-you email. If someone connected you with the person, send a thank-you email to the person who connected you, telling them how much you appreciate them making the connection and how much you enjoyed talking to the other person.

The best networking interactions are reciprocal. If you were able to offer anything to them during the conversation, like an introduction, or mentioned something you thought they might like (e.g. an article, book, podcast), include the link or thing in the thank-you email. It's always nice to give something back to someone who has so generously shared their time with you—and can help build a relationship.

Additionally, if you feel like the conversation went well, connect with the person on LinkedIn.

Sometimes, people will tell you to reach out if you need anything else or to let them know what job you end up taking. If you felt that you built a good connection, take them up on their offer or let them know where you land. This can be an opportunity to form a long-term relationship.

6. APPLYING

THE STRATEGY OF GETTING A JOB YOU LOVE

Early in her search, Olivia scoured the internet late one night and dropped her resume for twenty open positions. While she wasn't very interested in several of the roles, it felt like progress. A few days later, she received an interview; a week after that, she received an offer with a deadline of one week to decide. Sounds great, right?

Maybe. But, since she hadn't applied to the places she really wanted to work, she faced a tough decision. Should she take the job, or decline it and try to get a job at one of her top choices? She ultimately turned down the offer but wondered: *Have I shut a door that I might want to be open later?*

To get a job you love, you must be strategic in your application process.

Don't apply for any jobs you find. Instead, take the time to develop an application strategy, as outlined in this chapter. Below, we will discuss how to find jobs, how to apply in a way that is more likely to get interviews—and even how to create your own job.

So, how do you start? First, make a list of *all* the companies you are interested in. Think back to your networking conversations—and refer to your <u>Networking Tracker</u> from the *Art of the Job Search* website. Based on what you know now, what companies sound the most interesting? Write them down. This list can also include companies where you haven't networked with anyone who works there.

Next, rank your list of companies using a very simple system:

- A = Best. You would *love* to work there.
- B = Better. You would like to work there, but not as much as at your A companies.
- C = Good. You would like to work there, but not as much as your A or B companies.

The strategy is simple: Apply to jobs you really want at your 'A' companies first.

Apply to jobs you *really* want first—the ones you would take if you got an offer.

Remember Olivia's story? You don't want to have to decide on an offer when you aren't sure if you could get a job at one of your top companies.

What if you need interview practice? Prepare by practicing with someone, like a partner or a friend. Use the tips on preparing for interviews from Chapter 7. Your networking conversations will also help you prepare for interviews—and make you more comfortable talking to people you don't already know.

When you're ready to apply to your A companies, apply to several at once. Apply in batches based on your level of interest. For example, if there are fifty jobs on your list, rank them by interest level. If there are ten that you are most interested in, apply to these first.

Why? Because if you get an offer, you will have a very short period of time to decide if you want to accept—often just one week. So, apply first to the things you most want.

Why are decision periods often so short? Usually, the position is already vacant, and the company is desperate to get someone in the door—because work isn't getting done, or because someone is doing two jobs.

WHERE TO FIND (GREAT) JOBS

So, how do you find jobs that interest you? Here are some great sources:

- **Friends and Acquaintances**: Continue to tell people that you are searching. Fifty percent of open jobs are not publicly posted, and new jobs emerge all the time. By reminding people what you are searching for, you can become top of mind when someone learns that their company is hiring for your dream job—whether it's posted or not.

- **Company Websites**: Many company websites list open jobs at the company. (Though you can submit your resume online, sending it directly to person at the company is almost always more effective—more on this below.)

- **Alumni School Job Boards**: Check your alumni job boards. There are often good opportunities posted here, not to mention that you already have something in common: your alma mater.

- **LinkedIn:** LinkedIn also has job postings and groups, both of which are worth searching. It's easy to apply via LinkedIn for these roles as well.

- **Job Aggregation Sites:** On sites like Indeed and ZipRecruiter, you can enter custom searches and receive daily emails listing jobs that match your criteria.

- **Glassdoor:** Glassdoor is a great resource for understanding what it's like inside a company, providing salary information and ratings from actual employees. It also includes a job board with open opportunities.

- **Vocate:** If you are a student, Vocate is a great free resource that can help you explore your interests, build valuable job-search skills, and ultimately match you with the right opportunities—both internships and full-time positions.

- **Headhunters:** Headhunters are especially useful when you are seeking a similar position to the one you had. If you are industry or role-switching, headhunters may be a less productive source, as they often look for candidates with directly relevant experience for their roles.

HOW TO APPLY (AND GET AN INTERVIEW)

When I was hiring for a role on my team, over 172 candidates submitted resumes online—but I only saw fifty of them. Why? Our system required me to download each resume one-by-one from the system—and I didn't have time. So, I never saw 70 percent of the resumes that candidates submitted online for my roles.

It never hurts to submit a resume online. Who knows, you might be the lucky 30 percent? But to give yourself the best chance of getting an interview, apply through a person at the company.

Who should you ask? Remember those people that you networked with who said they'd be happy to help you? Do you have any friends who work at the company? Or friends of friends? You can ask any of these people to send your resume to the hiring manager for the role you are interested in.

If you don't think you know anyone at the company, search LinkedIn. You may find that you have second or third degree connections. Try to connect with these people through your friends. Email your friend telling them that you are thinking of applying to the company and would love to chat with their friend to get their perspective on the company and role.

Applying through a person, versus an online system, is *infinitely* more effective.

THREE REASONS TO APPLY THROUGH A PERSON
(Versus an online system)

- **Your resume goes directly to the hiring manager.**
  Your resume bypasses HR and goes straight to the person you would be working for if hired. If they think you could be a match, they often will move to get you in the door for an interview much faster.

- **You are now a personal recommendation.**
  When your resume comes gets submitted by someone internally, you become a personal recommendation—and these are powerful. Think about what it's like when you meet a friend of a friend. Your friend has likely said great things about their friend, so it's almost like you are already friends when you meet. The same thing happens in the recruiting process. If you are referred by someone internally, then you already have a connection before you walk in the door. They already *want* to like you.

- **Your resume is now *actually* reaching someone.**
  By sending your resume to a person, you ensure that it's not trapped inside the online resume black box—which it may never leave.

Let's talk about the best way to make the ask. A common mistake people make is sending an email to a networking connection that looks something like this:

BAD EXAMPLE EMAIL
(*Situation*: Asking someone to submit your resume)

Hi Mark,

Great to chat recently. I'm applying to the Marketing Manager role at your company. Would you mind sending my resume (attached) to the hiring manager?

Thanks,
Mari

This email is misses a major opportunity. Mark will most likely forward this email directly to hiring manager. Where's the information about Mari? What qualifications does she bring? Why is she interested in the role?

Email is now starting to take the place of a cover letter, so a great email looks something like a slightly less formal version of a cover letter. It is clear, concise and professional—and free of typos and grammatical errors. A great email also conveys gratitude since you are essentially asking the person to vouch for your candidacy to their colleagues.

These are the essential pieces of information to include in an effective ask:

- Relevant experience
- Interest in the role / enthusiasm
- Link to the job for which you're applying
- Resume in PDF

Here is a good sample email:

GOOD EXAMPLE EMAIL
(*Situation*: Asking someone to submit your resume)

Hi Mark,

Thanks again for chatting with me a couple weeks ago. I am really excited about the Digital Strategy Manager role on the Innovation & Strategy team, and I am planning to apply: [Insert Job Link]. **Is there any chance you could send my resume (attached) to the hiring manager?**

Here's a description of my experience and interest in the role in case it's helpful:

Mari Quinn is looking to transition from management consulting into digital strategy. Most recently, she worked at Accenture, where she worked on a digital strategy project for a Fortune 500 consumer company that resulted in a 30 percent increase in annual revenues. She received an MBA from New York University and a BA in Marketing from Arizona State University.

Thank you,
Mari

Attachment: Resume

Ensure that your resume follows the conventions discussed in this book and that you include a compelling Six-Second Summary, which will give you the best chance for getting an interview.

If you don't hear back within a week or two, follow up.

CAN'T FIND THE RIGHT ROLE? CREATE IT

A common misconception that people have is that their world of opportunity is limited to posted jobs. But it's endless—if you're willing to take a different approach.

Mina decided that she wanted to establish a marketing team at an early-stage startup. She identified five companies where she wanted to work—and checked their job postings. But none had open jobs.

So, she reached out to the CEOs to highlight her interest in founding their marketing team, her qualifications and what she could specifically do for each company. (How did she find their email addresses? She guessed. She found the company address on their "Contact Us" page, e.g., info@redblue.com. Then, she just tried different combinations of first and last name @redblue.com until the email went through.)

Guess what happened? All five CEOs responded and asked to have coffee with her. During her meeting with each CEO, she discussed what she could bring and what she was looking for—and ultimately got an offer at one of these companies.

Were there tradeoffs? Of course. While she negotiated a higher salary, she took a step back in terms of title and worked at "an ugly office with a co-ed bathroom and a bunch of 22-year-olds in hoodies." And she loved it. The culture was fun—and she gained valuable skills and experience building a marketing team from scratch. She was successful, too. In four years, she was promoted three times and built a marketing team of thirty people.

After four years, Mina gained the experience she sought and decided to move on again. She took a similar approach in her next search—and once again, created a job at one of her target companies.

Mina created her own opportunities—ones that she loved. If you're creative like this, who knows what can happen?

COMMON QUESTIONS

Can you apply to multiple roles at the same company?

Yes, unless explicitly stated otherwise. Most companies recognize that you have talents that could be valuable in different areas of the organization.

Should you disclose that you applied to multiple positions at the same company?

For smaller companies, disclose upfront that you applied to multiple positions. For larger companies, if you have applied to multiple positions, it's probably not necessary. But if you have had a conversation, like a phone screening or even a preliminary informational interview, disclose this *immediately* to the HR teams or hiring managers. If you receive an interview in more than one group, let them both know immediately as well.

Should you apply to multiple companies at once, even if you are only interested in one company?

Yes. If there are only one or two companies on your A list, apply to other jobs as well—from lower on your list. Why? Because it's important to find the right match—and if you get other offers, this gives you the strongest negotiating position.

Should you apply to <u>any</u> job at your A companies?

Apply *only* for roles that you are interested in and that meet your criteria, as defined by the self-assessment you took in Chapter 2.

There's a decent job at a B or C company now. What if it's gone by the time you're ready to apply to B or C companies?

This is a common concern. But, wouldn't it be worse to know that you took a B or C option without knowing if you could get one of your A jobs? You will find the right role—it's possible that it's not even available yet.

How do you manage companies working on different hiring timelines?

Let's say you get an offer from Company X that expires in one week. You have two other interviews lined up that aren't happening until *after* your deadline to respond to Company X. What should you do?

Reach out to the two companies. Tell them you have an expiring offer, and ask if they can move up your interviews. Be tactful, but don't be afraid to be honest about timelines. Try to move the interview up to the soonest date possible so you have time to weigh your options if you get multiple offers. Most often, companies will move your interview. The thought that you *might* take a job elsewhere can be very motivating.

7. INTERVIEW PREPARATION

HOW TO INTERVIEW INCREDIBLY WELL

Early in my career, I dreaded presenting in leadership meetings. But not Zeb, who was the same level as me, and almost as confident as our CEO.

I assumed that he was born with amazing communication skills until late one night at the office, when I saw him in a conference room practicing his presentation for the next day. Over and over— and over again.

In that moment, I realized that Zeb developed his communication skills, with lots of practice. I also realized that I could do that too—if I put in the time and effort.

So, before my next presentation, I rehearsed for hours on end. Afterwards, I received unsolicited positive feedback from several people regarding my presentation. Like Zeb, I invested the time to build the skill—and it paid off.

The same principal applies to interviewing.

Strong interview skills are *built* through practice and preparation.

Recently, I asked people working at top companies, like Google, Facebook, and other Fortune 500 companies, to describe their interview approach. How did they get their jobs?

One thing was consistent: they prepared for their interviews—thoroughly. One described his interview preparation as "a rigorous process, where I learn the company inside and out." Each person followed a very similar three-step process:

- **Research** the company and industry
- **Prepare** interview answers and questions
- **Practice** for the interview

In this chapter, we will talk about how to do each of these things, and we will go into specifics, like how to answer questions like: "What's your greatest weakness?" For each of your interviews, create a separate <u>Interview Sheet</u>, using the guidance below on how to fill out each section.

What happens if you spend a lot of time preparing—and still don't get the job? (It's probably going to happen.) Try to have a growth mindset, as discussed in Chapter 3. Instead of viewing your interview as a failure, ask yourself the following questions:

- What did you learn?
- What could you have done differently?
- How will you apply your learnings in your next interview?

Then, keep on interviewing and pursuing roles you really want—and remember that there is something amazing out there for you.

FIRST STEP? PREPARE & RESEARCH THE COMPANY

One question Ava always asked candidates was "Why do you want to work at our company?"

The most common answer people gave was, "I love their clothes!" While this was likely true, it was not unique. So, imagine how impressive it was when a candidate said, "I'm interested in your technological innovation in fabrics," before proceeding to describe her passion for the work and how she could contribute to it.

She had done her research, and Ava was impressed—so much that she remembers this candidate's answer three years later.

Researching the company enables you to give better answers *and* ask insightful questions.

There are three main types of information to obtain in advance of your interview, which we will discuss in depth below:

- Company Information
- Inside Insights
- Interviewer Information

THREE TYPES OF INFORMATION TO GATHER

1. Company Information

You don't need to memorize key facts and figures. Instead, try to learn some general information that will enable you to ask insightful questions about the company. If the company is public, read the most recent quarterly earnings transcript, which you can find on Seeking Alpha. In this report, the CEO discusses top priorities, key challenges, and growth opportunities. (If you are pressed for time and can only do one thing, read the quarterly earnings transcript.)

You don't need to be a financial genius to understand the quarterly reports. The CEO comments at the beginning are usually easy to understand. Not to mention that it's pretty impressive to say in an interview, "I was looking at your most recent earnings transcript and saw that Jeff Bezos said . . . "

Below is the data to include on your Interview Sheet for each company—and where to find it.

INTERVIEW SHEET

Company Information
(Sources of information in italics)

Key Facts
- Brief company history—date founded, key changes *(Company Website, Wikipedia)*
- CEO *(Company Website, Wikipedia)*
- Key facts—e.g., brands, clients *(Company Website, Wikipedia)*
- Revenue *(10K or Yahoo Finance!)*
- Recent news *(Google, Quarterly Earnings Transcript—Seeking Alpha)*

Opportunities
- Key opportunities/growth areas *(Quarterly Earnings Transcript—Seeking Alpha)*
- Ideas for growth

Challenges
- Key challenges *(Quarterly Earnings Transcript—Seeking Alpha)*
- Key competitors *(Quarterly Earnings Transcript—Seeking Alpha, Yahoo Finance!)*
- Ideas for how to combat competitive threats

Industry Information

- Top industry news *(Industry Newsletters, Google)*
- Top competitor news *(Industry Newsletters, Google)*
- Industry innovation—e.g., product, shipping, customer experience, digital *(Google, Industry Newsletters)*

2. Inside Insights

One of the best resources for getting insights into the company and role is by talking to people affiliated with the company. These can include: current employees, past employees, partners, and clients.

Conversations with people affiliated with the company can help you answer important questions like: What is the manager like? What does the role *really* entail? Is the group's work valued internally? What does the future of the company and/or group look like?

Another benefit of talking to someone in advance is that they often put in a good word for you with the interviewers. Almost every time I've spoken to someone at the company in advance of my interview, I'm greeted with something like "You're a friend of Ben's—welcome."

Professors Tanya Menon and Leigh Thompson describe this as the *connection effect*:

If you can find even one point of commonality in few moments of interacting, you can shift from outsider to insider in the interviewer's mind. As an insider, you'll receive the benefit of the doubt, as compared to an outsider who's quickly judged and dismissed.

Below are some sample questions to ask during your conversations. Use your judgement, and ask what feels appropriate.

INSIDE INSIGHTS QUESTIONS

Company Questions
- Can you tell me about your experience at the company?

- What are the current priorities?
- What are the major growth areas?
- Can you describe the culture?

Team/Role Questions

- What projects are the team currently working on?
- What are they looking for in a candidate?
- Can you tell me about the manager?
- Why did the prior person leave this role?
- Have there been any major changes on the team?

Interview Questions

- What can I expect in the interview?
- Can you describe your interview experience?
- Is there a case interview? Can you describe how it works?
- Do you have any tips for the interview?
- Can you tell me more about the interviewers?
- Anything else I should know?

You may receive some surprising answers to these questions, like "the manager has a bad reputation," or "the group was recently reorganized, and it's a mess." No position is perfect—and remember, this is one person's opinion. After your conversation, determine what questions you still need answered to determine if you want the job—and ask them during your interview if it feels appropriate. (If it doesn't feel appropriate to ask these questions, you will have another opportunity to ask questions to people on the team if you get the offer.)

The people you talk to do not need to be on the same team or work in the same division in which you are interviewing. It's often better when they are not, as an outsider can provide a more unbiased perspective. Past employees are also a great resource.

If you really don't know anyone, skip this step. But if you have *any* connection at the company, reach out. The connection effect is powerful.

3. Interviewer Information

In advance of the interview, use Google and LinkedIn to gather information about your interviewers. If you don't have a list of your interviewers, email your HR contact, and ask if they can send you the names of the people on your interview panel. (If you are using LinkedIn, you can change your settings to "anonymous" so they cannot see that you looked at their profiles.)

Building on the power of the connection effect, try to figure out if you have anything in common with your interviewers. Did they go to the same school as you? Did they work at a same company?

If you don't find anything in advance, try to find something during the interview. Scan your interviewer's desk—what do you have in common? Maybe a favorite sports team? Maybe you both have kids? If you can, try to connect over these shared interests in the small talk before the interview begins.

THE INTERVIEW PROCESS

Often, companies follow a similar interview process, as outlined in Appendix B—a phone screening, a first-round interview, and then the final-round interview. But not always.

I was chatting with a friend recently who had just finished what she thought was the final round of interviews. When the company called her afterwards, she was surprised—they invited her for a *third* round of interviews.

How do you avoid this surprise? If you are unclear on any part of the interview process, ask the recruiter what to expect.

Questions you can ask include:

1. How does the interview process work?
2. How many rounds of interviews do you conduct?

3. How long will I meet with each person?

4. How many people will I be meeting with?

5. Can you give me the names of the interviewers?

6. Do you conduct case interviews?

7. Is there anything that I should prepare in advance?

You do not need to ask all these questions. But if you find yourself confused about any of these things during the process: ask. You can call the recruiter—or send them an email if it's a less urgent or less complicated question.

WHAT IS A GREAT INTERVIEW ANSWER?

What is a good interview answer? In one word: memorable. See below for four ways to give great interview answers.

4 WAYS GIVE GREAT INTERVIEW ANSWERS

1. Be concise.

In one interview that Martin conducted, the candidate took fifteen minutes to answer each question. Since the entire interview was thirty-minutes, he was only able to ask two questions—and did not get enough information to hire the candidate.

So, what should be the maximum length for an answer? Two minutes. If your interviewer wants to know more, they'll ask.

2. Give structured answers.

Speak in bullet points. For example, "Based on feedback I've received, I have three top strengths: 1) executive communication, 2) a strategic approach to problem solving, and 3) finding creative solutions." Then, proceed to describe each in more detail.

Using bullet points has three key advantages. It will make your answers 1) structured, 2) concise, and 3) memorable.

3. Talk about what _you_ did.

One of the most common mistakes people make in interviews is answering with "we." Here's an example:

Question: *Tell me about a time you had to influence someone at work.*

Bad Answer: *Well, there was a woman, Grace, who wasn't on board with the customer satisfaction survey that we wanted to conduct. So, we figured out why and addressed her concerns. And she let us conduct the survey, which gave us insights enabling us to increase customer satisfaction by 30 percent.*

Okay, sounds like your team was successful. That's great. But what did _you_ specifically do? Here's a great answer to the same question, one that illuminates what you specifically did, while also acknowledging the team.

Interviewer: Tell me about a time you had to influence someone at work.

Good Answer: Well, there was this woman, Grace, who wasn't on board with the customer satisfaction survey that we wanted to conduct. I realized that it was important to figure out why, so I scheduled a one-on-one meeting to address her concerns. By talking through it, I realized that she didn't like a few of the questions. So, we removed three questions, had her review it again—and she agreed to let us send it out. Once we received the results, I analyzed them and made recommendations to the leadership team on what to change. They agreed with three of my top recommendations, and I worked with Grace to implement them. This led to a 30 percent increase in customer satisfaction in the past year.

This is a nice answer. It acknowledges other people and their contributions while focusing on what you specifically did.

4. Don't caveat your answers.

I was recently working with someone looking to change careers. She didn't have experience in the new industry—and felt like she needed to explicitly highlight her gaps in her interview.

It's assumed that you will have to learn new things when you take a new job. So, don't sell yourself short. If you get the job, you will learn what you need to succeed in the role. And if you really don't feel like you can learn the skills, then don't apply.

HOW TO ANSWER THE MOST IMPORTANT QUESTION

"Walk me through your resume."

How often have you been asked this question? It's usually the first question in every interview. You sit down, and the interviewer starts with this seemingly simple warm-up question.

It is a warm-up question, right? Research would indicate otherwise. According to recent studies, most interviewers make a hiring decision in the first seven minutes of your interview. Once you've finished the small talk and answered this question, your seven minutes are almost up.

So, this seemingly innocuous question is *the most important question* of the entire interview—and it's also the most commonly messed up question.

Usually, people approach it chronologically: "Well, I was born in Marfa, Texas and lived there for eighteen years until I went to college at the University of Texas. Then, I started by majoring in English but then switched to Biology . . . " That's interesting, but it doesn't tell your interviewer much about why you are qualified for the job.

Interviewers are usually looking for three specific things:

- **Relevant experience**
- **Interest** in the job
- **Communication skills**—and an ability to be concise

The ideal way to answer this question is to identify the themes in your background that make you well qualified for the role—and then to talk about a few specific, relevant experiences. Your answer to this question should be two minutes, maximum. Practice this answer until you are satisfied with it—because you will get this question in almost every interview you have.

Here is how I answered the question when I was interviewing for a digital strategy role at a retailer, where the job description said they sought: retail experience, problem-solving skills, creativity, and strategic thinking.

Question: *Walk me through your background.*

Answer: *When I look back at my experiences, I realize that they reflect a passion for problem-solving, creativity, and strategic thinking, all of which seem critical for this role. After receiving my MBA at Stanford, I joined Boston Consulting Group, which enabled me to utilize my strategic skills to solve problems for several Fortune 500 companies. My favorite project involved working with an underperforming retailer to optimize their online presence to enable them to better compete in today's digital world. Prior to receiving my MBA, I worked at Goldman Sachs in real estate private equity, where a primary component of my job was developing strategic initiatives to enhance performance of the hotels I worked on. I also received a Master's in Art History, which reflects my passion for creativity. I look forward to using my strategic problem-solving and creativity, and to leverage my retail experience in my next role.*

What I did not include in this answer are all my irrelevant experiences: working in the oil and gas industry, a project at a dairy company, an internship at an educational non-profit, majoring in French, volunteering with kids, being a member of the wine club in business school. I included only the relevant experiences for the specific job—and practiced my answer extensively.

Now, create your own. Remember: two minutes maximum and practice a lot.

COMMON QUESTIONS (AND HOW TO ANSWER THEM)

Below, you will find other commonly asked interview questions—and guidance on how to answer them. In most interviews, you will probably get these questions—or some version of them. So, prepare your answers, and practice them.

COMMON INTERVIEW QUESTIONS
(And how to answer them)

QUESTION 1: Why do you want this job?
(Alternative: Why do you want to work at this company?)

Caroline, a hiring manager at a top consulting company, said that she's surprised how many candidates botch this question. Often, people will say that "they want to learn." While that's almost always true, the company is much more interested in what you bring them versus what they can teach you.

So, what's a good answer?

A good answer conveys the skills that you *bring* to the role, specific knowledge of the company and enthusiasm—about the industry, company, and work. Here's an example:

Question: Why are you interested in working here?

Bad Answer: I really like clothes and want to learn more about retail. Also, I shopped at your company a lot in high school. I remember buying my first day of junior high outfit there, so this company is special to me.

Good Answer: To start, I'm impressed by the innovative, customer-centric approach this company is taking that is unique in retail, like the investment in a new mobile app and testing products directly with customers. I would love to use my strategy experience to help you innovate and transform the industry. [Include a couple more reasons with specific examples—e.g., culture, other initiatives.]

QUESTION 2: What are your strengths?

The best answers are structured, concise, and involve strengths that are applicable to the specific role. Aim for three strengths to keep your answer concise. Additionally, try to use feedback and evidence in your answers.

Question: *What are your strengths?*

Bad Answer: *I'm good at strategy, communication, and management. I enjoy managing teams and think it's fun to engage with people.* [This answer lacks specificity and objective data. See below for a better answer.]

Good Answer: *I've received feedback that my key strengths are managing teams, executive communication, and strategy. Recently, I managed a team of seven people and was ranked in the top 10 percent of managers across the entire company. I strongly believe in feedback as a tool in developing people and ensure that I have a weekly discussion with each member of my team . . .* [Then, elaborate on each of your other strengths in the same way.]

QUESTION 3: What are your weaknesses?

This is probably one of your least favorite questions, and it's also one that you will likely be asked. Here are a couple suggestions for answering this question:

- **Do not use a critical weakness.** Do not give a weakness that would prevent you from doing the job effectively.

- **Show your ability to improve.** Ideally, choose something that you struggled with in the past, talk about the steps you took to improve it, and the positive result of your efforts.

Interviewer: *What's your greatest weakness?*

Bad Answer: *I've been told that I struggle with confidence in my* *presentations. I really hate presenting in front of other people. It makes me nervous.*

Good Answer: *In the past, I struggled with presenting to large groups, and I really wanted to improve this skill. So, I took presentation classes and asked my manager for an opportunity to present our project findings to a large team. I practiced extensively before the big presentation, which went well according to my manager. I then continued to seek opportunities to improve this skill—and recently received positive feedback in my recent annual review regarding my presentation skills.*

Have a couple examples like this ready, because often people ask for multiple weaknesses. Your interviewer may follow up and ask what a *current* weakness is. Do *not* give a critical weakness that would seem to prevent you from doing the job well, and discuss the current steps you are taking to improve this weakness.

BEHAVIORAL QUESTIONS

Behavioral interview questions are increasingly common and go something like this: "Tell me about a time when . . . "

- You worked with a difficult person.
- You had to influence someone.
- You had to bring people together to accomplish an objective.

These questions sound challenging, but there's a good framework to use to answer them: the STAR method.

STAR METHOD
(For "Tell me about a time when…" questions)

Situation
Start by giving a brief overview of the situation. What was the

challenge you faced? (Keep it to one or two sentences maximum.)

Task

Describe the task you were responsible for. What was your specific role?

Action

What was the action you took? What did *you* specifically do? What did you learn?

Result

What was the outcome? How did you specifically contribute?

Keep your answers concise—no more than three minutes. Prepare your answers in advance, and practice them.

How do you prepare examples if the questions could be different? Here's the thing: the questions are usually very similar—a time when you had a problem, steps you took to solve the problem, and the results. So, all you really need is a few good examples.

So, prepare a few different stories of when you faced challenges at work. These will likely be applicable for the questions you are asked.

Here's a good example of using the STAR method from an earlier example in the book.

Question: *Tell me about a time you had to influence someone at work.*

Good Answer: *Well, there was this woman, Grace, who wasn't on board with the customer satisfaction survey that we wanted to conduct. I realized that it was important to figure out why, so I scheduled a one-on-one meeting to address her concerns. By talking through it, I realized that she didn't like a few of the questions. So, we removed three questions, had her review it again—and she agreed to let us send it out. Once we received the results, I analyzed them and made recommendations to the leadership team on what to change. They agreed with three of my top recommendations,* *and I worked with Grace to implement them. This led to a 30 percent increase in customer satisfaction in the past year.*

CASE INTERVIEWS

These are a key component of management consulting interviews, and case interviews are becoming more common across other industries as well. If you are preparing for a management consulting interview, here are my top recommendations from my experience at Boston Consulting Group: buy a case book like *Case in Point*, study it, and find a case partner to practice with weekly. Also, try to practice a few times with ex-consultants. They can give you the best feedback since they know *exactly* what your interviewers are seeking.

If you are interviewing at other types of companies, try to figure out if they ask case interview questions and what they entail. You can ask the HR representative if you should be prepared to do a case interview, and you can ask friends at the company about how the case interviews work. You can also check Glassdoor to see if there are any examples of past case questions people were asked.

Then, prepare and practice your case interviews. If you can, try to practice cases with employees or ex-employees of the company.

PROJECTS OR PRESENTATIONS

Projects are becoming increasingly common because they enable interviewers to gauge several things at once: communication skills, work quality, and how interested the candidate is in the job. So, if the company requires a project and you really want the job, prepare extensively. A friend recently put twenty hours into preparing for his interview project.

You won't always get the job, even when you spend a lot of time preparing. But if you really want something, put the effort in. Even if you don't get the job, you will likely learn something in the process of doing the project that will be useful for future interviews.

NEXT STEP? PRACTICE.

Write out bullet point answers to all the interview questions above. You can use the <u>Interview Questions</u> template on the *Art of the Job Search* website. I recommend bullet points versus writing your answers with sentences. Bullet points will give you key talking points that make your answers seem natural, not memorized or overly rehearsed.

In addition to the questions in this chapter, try to anticipate and prepare for other interview questions you might be asked. See Appendix A for a long list of common interview questions. And do some online research on websites like Glassdoor to see what types of questions the specific company usually asks.

Then, practice—a lot. Practice in your bathroom mirror. Practice in the car when you're driving to work. Practice in an empty conference room. Then, try to practice with others—perhaps with a good friend or partner. If you really want to improve, ask them for feedback. Specifically, ask:

- Are your answers clear?
- Are they concise? (i.e. Two minutes or less?)
- Do you seem polished, but not overly rehearsed?
- Are there any verbal distractions? (e.g., too many "ums" or "likes")
- Were there any non-verbal distractions? (e.g., brushing hair aside)
- Any other recommendations?

8. INTERVIEWING

THE #1 INTERVIEW SECRET

During business school, I applied to tons of internships—and only received one offer. So, I asked a friend who had gotten offers at investment banks, consulting firms and technology companies: what was his secret?

He shared this life-changing piece of wisdom:

Act like you are interviewing them.

Wait . . . *what?*

I initially thought his advice was crazy. Then, I tried it—and started receiving more offers. After taking this approach, I realized that it made sense for two key reasons.

1. It shows confidence and ownership.

In a recent survey of top managers asking what they seek in job candidates, they revealed: "We want people who are problem solvers and are willing to take initiative. We want people . . . who act like they own the place." Turns out, ownership and confidence are two of the top traits that hiring managers seek. What better way to show these qualities than in your interview style?

2. You *should* be interviewing them.

Most people approach the interview as a one-sided thing: they need to impress the company. But you *should* be interviewing the company too. Even if the company really wants you, do *you* actually want to work there? The interview is a key opportunity to figure this out.

HOW TO 'ACT LIKE YOU ARE INTERVIEWING THEM'

So, there are benefits to acting like you are interviewing them, but how do you do it? There are a few critical ways.

5 WAYS TO 'ACT LIKE YOU ARE INTERVIEWING THEM'

1. Own the introduction.

First impressions are critical and often made in the first fifteen seconds of an interview. Often, people wait for the interviewer to initiate the handshake and conversation. But *you* should do this instead. Each time you meet someone new, stand up and offer your hand first—and give a solid handshake. Ask a rapport-building question like "How's your day going?" or "How was your weekend?" Be enthusiastic, and smile.

Not only does this approach show your interviewers that you are confident, but also it sets you up for success by *making* you more confident. Acting confident can lead to actual confidence—which will make you more effective in the rest of the interview.

2. Ask more questions.

In my failed job search, I viewed the interviewers as the

question-askers and myself as the question-answerer. I politely waited to speak until addressed—and this approach failed miserably.

Instead, make each interview a two-way dialogue by asking questions during the interview—from the moment it starts. This is the most effective way to 'act like you are interviewing them.'

Here are some questions you can ask during each phase of the interview:

- **Beginning**: Ask how they are doing when they sit down.
- **Middle**: Ask questions about the role or your interviewer's background. Ask questions that come up for you during the conversation.
- **End**: Ask good questions that you've prepared (see #5).

In one interview where I asked a ton of questions, the interviewer never got around to asking me a question. I led the conversation, and it ended up being a very casual, informative—and enjoyable—discussion. And, I got the job.

Interviewers were receptive to the two-way dialogue approach during about 80 percent of my interviews. But sometimes, more formal interviewers like to stick to their script. So, if you sense that the conversational approach is not working, let it go.

3. Form a connection.

At a past company, one of the factors we assessed in candidates was: "Would you want to be stuck in an airport with them for eight hours?" Because we travelled a lot—and it happened sometimes.

People hire people they like.

So, feel free to be yourself and show some personality. You don't always have to be serious in interviews. It's okay to laugh and enjoy the conversation. Take a cue from your interviewer—if they seem more relaxed, then you can be more informal as well.

4. Be confident.

It's hard to feel confident when you feel nervous. But it's possible—even more so when you've prepared and practiced. Anticipate what questions might be asked. Specifically, what questions could they ask that would make you nervous? Prepare and practice your answers to these using the tactics in Chapter 7.

A few other tips for exuding confidence: make eye contact, keep your answers concise, and cut the filler words, including "like" and "um."

5. Prepare good questions in advance.

Always be prepared to ask questions at the end of an interview. Asking questions demonstrates your interest in the role and that you're thinking about how you can contribute. Plus, it's your opportunity to continue to interview them.

Questions you can ask include the following:

- What are your top priorities right now?
- What are your goals for this year?
- What is your vision for this team in a year?
- What is the team structure?
- How does this role interact with other people on the team and at the company?
- Can you tell me about some of the projects that you are working on?
- What do you like most and least about working here?

To ask really impressive questions, brainstorm specific questions pertaining to the company or role that only your interviewer could answer.

PHONE AND VIDEO INTERVIEW ADVICE

Phone and video interviews are becoming more common. Usually your first-round interview will be over the phone. And these days, more final-round interviews are being conducted over video, especially if you live in a different location. Here are a few tips for phone and video interviews:

- **Prepare in advance.** Prepare just like you would for an in-person interview. Develop an <u>Interview Sheet</u>. Research the company beforehand. Prepare answers in advance, and practice them out loud.

- **Go to a private, quiet space.** Conduct your interview in a quiet room by yourself—it's less distracting for you and the person on the other end of the line. If you're at home, go to a private room, and shut the door. If you're at work, try to find an empty conference room or office.

- **Start with small talk.** Open the conversation with some small talk, which will help to build a connection, even when you aren't in the same physical place.

- **Have your Interview Sheet in front of you.** If it's a phone interview, you can have your <u>Interview Sheet</u> and resume in front of you to reference during the call.

- **Take notes.** Taking notes can be useful for the final-round interview. What you learn can help you tailor questions and answers for your next interview.

- **Don't stress about technical difficulties.** Sometimes, video cuts out or calls drop. Try to stay calm—and keep on going.

In addition to the above tips for phone interviews, here are a few more things to consider for video interviews:

- **Make sure the technology works.** If you haven't used the video on your computer, make sure it works beforehand. Test it out with a friend or family member.

- **Pay attention to lighting and background.** Check your background. Does it look acceptable? Try to sit in a clean area with good lighting.

- **Look at the camera.** Look at the camera on your computer, versus the person on the screen. It will look like you are making eye contact, versus looking down. A quick hack for making virtual eye contact with your interviewer is to place your computer slightly higher and level with your eyes. You can place your computer on a stack of books.

- **Dress like you would for an in-person interview.** The person can see you, so dress like you would for an in-person interview.

- **Smile and show enthusiasm.** Make sure you look enthusiastic—and engage with the person on the other end as if they were in the same room. Pay attention to your body language as well.

WHAT TO WEAR AND OTHER TIPS

How do you know what to wear? Ask. Check with your HR contact—or ask someone who works at the company. If it's a jeans-and-hoodie culture, you don't want to show up in a suit. If you are uncertain, lean towards being overdressed. It's better to be the one in business casual when your interviewers are wearing jeans, versus the other way around.

A note on being early. A lot of people advise you to arrive really early to an interview. While you can arrive as early as you'd like, don't check in until five minutes before the interview. Why? Because it can be annoying to your interviewer if they are called to come get you fifteen minutes before your interview.

Check the mirror before your interviews. Once you've arrived, go to the bathroom and take one last look. When Camille was interviewing candidates, there was one who had green leaves in her hair. It was so distracting that she had a hard time focusing on her answers. So, check your hair, your teeth, and your clothes when you arrive.

Be friendly to everyone you meet—from the security guard outside to the receptionist and assistants. At one startup, the assistant walks each interviewer to the conference room—and the CEO asks the assistant's opinion of each candidate. This is part of the interview. Not to mention that being nice is always the right thing to do.

THE BEST THANK-YOU EMAIL

Always send a thank-you note. It enables you to share your gratitude at being given the opportunity, and gives you one last chance to show why you are great for the job.

But do not send a handwritten note. While there's something great about a handwritten note in these days of technology-everything, mail is slow—and hiring decisions are often made quickly. If you send a note in the mail, it's possible it will arrive *after* the decision has been made.

Instead, use email for thank-you notes. Try to send your note the day of the interview. Ensure that it conveys your gratitude, references memorable things you discussed with each person, and talks about the contributions you could make in the role.

EXAMPLE EMAIL

(*Situation*: Thank you email after an interview)

Hi Erin,

I wanted to thank you for taking the time to meet with me on Friday. I really enjoyed our conversation about opportunities for growth provided by the recent acquisition, especially our discussions around the planned expansion in China this year.

It sounds like your team is working on some very interesting projects, and I would love to use my experience in digital marketing to help you expand your brand internationally and connect with a new customer base.

Have a wonderful week – and thanks again,
Evie

WHAT HAPPENS IF IT'S AWKWARD?

After leaving one of my first interviews during college, I got home and realized that there were some papers under my resume—and they weren't mine. It turned out that I had accidentally brought home the office vacation calendar. (This was back in the days when people still used paper to manage their schedules.)

I was convinced that my prospects for getting the job were over. After I returned the calendar, I stopped by my favorite ice cream shop and bought a pint in preparation for that rejection call. Surprisingly, it didn't come. They laughed as they mentioned the vacation calendar incident—and offered me the job. I thought I was the only one who had done something like this during a job interview—until I started talking to others.

There was my friend who flew to Boston for a final-round interview with his dream company. During lunch in the company cafeteria, which was part of the interview, he leaned against a napkin display. It tipped over, spilling hundreds of napkins across the floor in front of his entire interview panel. Instead of panicking, he made a joke: "Would you like a napkin? How about several?" His interviewer laughed. And the next day, he got an offer.

Then, there was the girl who had an eight-hour day of interviews for an investment bank. She got home, reached in her purse for her apartment key—and found the company's bathroom key. She returned it—and also got the job.

Unexpected things happen—and they are often funny in retrospect. As these stories prove, you can still get the job—and probably just added some humor to your interviewers' day.

9. THE CALL

THE DING: HOW TO RESPOND WHEN YOU DON'T GET THE JOB

While it's never enjoyable, you will likely receive a "thanks, but no thanks" phone call after an interview.

Even if you feel disappointed, try to remain professional and polite on the call. Why? Because you might have future interactions with them. The person might refer you for another job in the company. You might work for the company at some point in the future, or you might run into them at an industry networking event in a few months. The world can be a very small place.

Here's how to approach the call:

1. **Say "thank you."** Start by thanking them for giving you the opportunity to interview.

2. **Ask for feedback.** Getting feedback can help you improve your approach for future interviews. For example, a friend received feedback that her answers were too long, so she

practiced being more concise and received an offer shortly afterwards. After you get the news, say, "I would love feedback as I continue my search. Can you share feedback from my interviews?" Then, apply this feedback to your next interviews.

THE OFFER: HOW TO RESPOND WHEN YOU *DO* GET THE JOB

Congrats! You worked hard, the stars aligned—and you got the offer! Nice work. Before you grab a glass of champagne, think about how to approach the offer phone call. Your approach to the phone call can impact three important things, your: 1) reputation, 2) salary, and 3) career trajectory.

HOW TO APPROACH THE 'OFFER' CALL

- **Do *not* accept the offer on this call.** It's tempting to just say "yes!" when you receive the offer, but this prevents you from negotiating. So, listen to the offer and say thank you—but don't accept yet. In the meanwhile, read Chapter 10 for details on how to approach the negotiation.

- **Get the offer in writing.** *Always* get the offer in writing. A verbal offer is not binding. Getting the offer in writing will also enable you to assess your total compensation package and decide what you want to try to negotiate. Take a photo of the offer and save it in case you need to reference it in the future. You may even want the information for your next search.

- **Convey your gratitude and excitement.** Thank the company and communicate your excitement at being offered the role.

- **Determine the decision timeline.** Try to understand the deadline for your decision, and agree upon a date for them to send you the written offer.

Many companies give you no longer than a week to decide. While you can try to negotiate for a longer decision period, you may not be successful. So, start thinking about whether you want to take the job right after your call.

BUT, WAIT. DO YOU *WANT* THE JOB?

Before you accept the job, ask yourself the most important question: *do you want the job?* Re-read your self-assessment, and ask yourself:

- **Does the role align with your interests, values, and goals?** While nothing is perfect, seek to find a role that generally aligns with your self-assessment. Re-read the goals you set for your next position. Does this role align with those goals?

- **Does the job violate any deal-breakers?** If so, think very carefully. Unless there are extenuating circumstances, like financial need, or something can be negotiated, then the answer is no.

- **Do you want to work with the team? Did you feel at home in the culture?** People often underestimate the importance of these things. Working in a place where you feel comfortable makes it so much more enjoyable—and can lead to greater professional success.

Are there questions you need answered before you can decide

on the role? Ask them. Email HR and ask to set up a call with the members of the team who you think can best answer your questions. Once you have gotten your specific questions answered, ask yourself the most important questions:

- Overall, how do you feel about the position?
- Are you excited?
- Can you envision yourself working there?

When I took a prior role, the group was new and there was a lot that was undefined. But I really liked the team and was excited about the direction they were going. So, after talking to several members of the team, I trusted my instincts and took the role—and it was one of the best professional experiences I've had.

Here are two other questions to consider if they are important to you: Do you believe in the company's mission? Do you agree with how they are trying to achieve it?

Felix knew he wanted to work somewhere where he could positively impact the world. He found a for-profit company that was transforming the food space. Through his interviews, he discovered exactly what he was seeking, a "complete alignment between the social mission and the business." He took the job and has been there for the past five years.

Above all, remember: that a job is only great when it's a match on both sides.

10. NEGOTIATING

THE ($500K) COST OF NOT NEGOTIATING

People who don't negotiate miss out on $500k—or more—over their lifetime.

I initially doubted this, so I ran the numbers—and it really *is* true. If you just negotiated an extra $5,000 in your first job (e.g. from $50k to $55k), you would make an additional $504,607 over 50 years. (This assumes a 2.5 percent yearly salary increase, which is roughly equivalent to inflation.)

If you negotiated $10k in your first job (i.e. from $50k to $60k), that increases to over one million dollars of additional wages over your life. (You can see the calculation in the <u>Negotiation Calculator</u> on the website. You can also use this calculator to evaluate the lifetime value of your own negotiations.)

One million dollars! When I initially heard that figure, I thought: That's enough to pay for college—for five kids. Or to buy a house—and a vacation home. Or to provide two million meals to people who are hungry in the Bay Area.

When I got my first job out of college, I was so grateful that someone hired me that I couldn't imagine negotiating. So, I didn't try. I was afraid of what the company might think if I tried to negotiate. Would I seem ungrateful, confrontational, or entitled? What if they rescinded my job offer?

According to research, I wasn't alone. These fears are so common that only 37 percent of people say that they consistently negotiate salary. Women are four times less likely to negotiate than men—and when we do negotiate, we ask for less and receive 30 percent less than men.

Most employers expect candidates to negotiate. By not negotiating, you leave money on the table that the employer probably planned to pay you. After all, the company made you an offer because they really want you! They made only one offer—and that offer was extended to *you*.

When I extended offers, I usually wanted the person to accept the offer quickly for two reasons: 1) I liked them, and 2) the role was usually already vacant, so someone (often me) was doing two jobs. I wanted the candidate to take the role, because I didn't want to conduct another lengthy, time-consuming job search for several more months. So, I was usually motivated to negotiate if I could—and fast.

People are often concerned that by negotiating, they will set a bad tone. But, most hiring managers said that they viewed negotiating candidates even *more* favorably than those who do not negotiate, especially when it's done the right way—which we will discuss in this chapter.

Think about it: negotiation will likely be a skill you use in your job—to influence others and to get work done. By negotiating amicably using the tactics below, you are exhibiting your ability to succeed at your job, too.

HOW TO LEARN TO NEGOTIATE (EASILY)

So, how do you negotiate? I remember the first time I tried.

While shopping ten years ago, I found a cardigan that I really liked—with a broken button. I wanted it, but it seemed unreasonable to pay full price for a flawed product. So, when I checked out, I simply said, "This button is broken. Is there anything you can do?"

Without blinking, the cashier said, "Sure. 30 percent off." That was my first success, and it taught me four critical things about negotiation.

4 CRITICAL THINGS ABOUT NEGOTIATION

1. Learn to negotiate by starting with the small things.

Your first negotiation doesn't have to be your job offer or a raise. In fact, it's better if it's not. To build your skills, start small. Look for opportunities in everyday life to negotiate. Ask for a discount on a product, for two stamps on your coffee loyalty card, or for a discount on your car insurance. (Shop around for a better deal—and then see if your insurance will match it.)

Starting small helps build comfort with negotiating, which can enable greater confidence—and more success in future, larger negotiations, like a job offer or a raise.

2. Be nice.

Before I learned how to negotiate, I thought it would involve language like "I'm worth this" or "If you really wanted my business, you would give me 20 percent off." This type of approach is usually ineffective and simply makes the other person angry. According to Stanford professor Margaret Neale, taking the opposite approach generally leads to better outcomes:

> *When people cease to see negotiation as a fight, they open themselves up to more creative solutions and are able to see more situations as opportunities to negotiate.*

In other words, the best negotiations are done amicably, not in conflict. People are usually more willing to help the person who is nice. The best negotiations seek to agreeably come to a resolution that benefits both parties.

3. Frame it as a question.

Recently, I was purchasing some modern furniture and was hoping to get a lower price. So, I called the store and asked, "Is there a promotion going on right now?" The saleswoman said, "No, but I can offer you 20 percent off." Here's the lesson:

Negotiation is often as simple as asking a question.

Next time you are buying something, try to negotiate with a question. It's good practice for when you are negotiating larger things, like a job offer or a raise.

Here are some ideas for negotiating using questions:

- Is there a promotion going on right now? (If they say "no," try: "This is a large order—any chance you can offer 20 percent off?")
- I found the same product listed on Amazon for $X. Can you offer it at the same price?
- I noticed this small defect (if there is one)—can you offer a discount?
- I saw that you were offering X percent off last week—any chance that can be applied here?

4. Always Ask.

I'm shocked how many times I simply ask the question, and people unblinkingly say, "Yes." And when they say no, the relationship stays cordial. If you simply ask a question, how can they be upset with you?

So why does negotiation often work? Because there are usually benefits for both parties. In the sweater example, the store wanted me to purchase the item because they wanted my money, needed to sell the sweater to make room for more inventory, and perhaps because they saw it as an opportunity to create a loyal customer. And I wanted the sweater because I liked it—and because I wanted to feel like I got a good deal. In short:

Negotiation is often beneficial for both parties.

In your job search, the same principle applies. They really want you to work for them—and you want to be paid fairly. If you negotiate successfully, you both win. So, always ask—nicely.

3 BEST WAYS TO NEGOTIATE AN OFFER

The same principles for negotiating in your personal life apply to the job search. Negotiating your job offer doesn't need to be done in conflict. You can—and should—take an agreeable approach to negotiating your offer.

Here are the three best ways to *agreeably* negotiate your job offer.

3 BEST WAYS TO NEGOTIATE AN OFFER
(In an agreeable way)

1. Use other offers.

Regardless of whether you are going to take a job, negotiate the offer. Why? Because you can use this offer to negotiate other offers.

August used this approach and negotiated each offer that she received, even when she was not planning to take the job. When August finally got an offer for her dream job, she was told, "The max we can pay is $100,000. Final offer." Because she had data from other firms, she could confidently say, "I really want to work with you, but I received two other offers at a 20 percent higher salary." Two days later, they came back and matched her other offers with

$120,000, a salary they originally said was impossible.

2. Use personal reasons.

I was chatting with a friend recently who received an offer and wasn't sure if he could make ends meet financially if he took the job. His wife was currently unemployed, and they were expecting a baby. "But I can't tell them these things," he said.

Why not? Of course, you can—and should.

Recruiters are human too. They understand if you need more money to support your family. So, if there are personal reasons why you seek a higher salary, tell them.

3. Use data from other companies.

If you don't have other offers or personal reasons, you can use data. I recommend using data when you don't have competing offers, which tend to be the most palatable and effective way to negotiate salary. If you are using a personal reason, I recommend starting with the personal reason and using data as a backup.

If you take the data approach, try to find salaries for comparable positions to yours. A great source for salary data is Glassdoor, which includes thousands of companies and salaries for specific roles.

Another effective way to obtain salary information is through recruiters and headhunters trying to fill open jobs. Take their calls, and ask for the role's compensation package, including salary, bonus, and stock options—even if you do not have interest in the role. This will help you figure out your market value—what other companies are willing to pay you.

(Keeping track of your market value while employed is a good practice. It can help you negotiate during a promotion or a year-end review. So, keep taking headhunter calls while employed, even if you don't intend to switch roles.)

One more approach: ask friends in similar roles what range they would expect for the role. One thing I have observed over the course of my career is that men share salary data with each other *much* more often than women do, which could be one of the many contributing factors to the gender pay gap.

Clearly, it's hard to ask others to share salary data, so think about who you ask and how you frame the request. You could say something like, "I received an offer, and I'm trying to figure out if it's in line with the market. Since you've been in the industry for a few years, I was wondering if you could help by letting me know what the range you'd expect for this position is based on your experience? And no worries at all if you'd rather not discuss salaries—completely understand."

Once you figure out what the market value for the role is, it's important to consider how you present this data. What's *not* effective is saying things like "I found online that you pay other managers $10,000 more than what you offered me," or "My friend said that you pay her $78,000."

Instead, try to frame it in a more agreeable way, like: "I am so excited about this role and really want to work with you. I also want to ensure that the compensation is in line with the role. I have done a lot of research and found that other comparable positions pay around $70,000. Do you think you can offer something similar?"

WHAT ELSE CAN YOU NEGOTIATE?

It's always ideal to negotiate your base salary since it's subject to annual salary increases. But sometimes companies are legitimately unable to offer you a higher base salary when you take the job. This doesn't mean that all negotiation is off the table.

Get creative. There are other things you can negotiate. One friend really wanted time off between jobs. So, she negotiated to delay her start date—by two months. And she had some amazing travel experiences, backpacking through the Philippines, Indonesia, and Japan with her boyfriend.

Given that the role was already vacant, someone was probably doing two jobs. So, why did they let her delay her start date? As one hiring manager said, "It's *really* hard to find good people." This often enables you to negotiate.

If companies cannot negotiate base salary, they still may be able to offer an additional monetary incentive like a signing bonus (e.g. a one-time cash payment). Things you can negotiate include the following:

- Salary
- Job Title
- Annual bonus
- Signing bonus
- Relocation bonus
- Stock options/equity
- Vacation days
- Flexible hours
- Working from home
- Delayed start date
- Health coverage
- Reimbursements (tuition, daycare, etc.)

Of course, don't negotiate all these things. Instead, think about what is most important to you and negotiate accordingly—ideally just a few things.

YOUR NEXT NEGOTIATION

A common perspective is that once you've accepted the job, you're done negotiating. While it is easiest to negotiate before you take a job (so *always* try to negotiate your initial job offer), continue to look for opportunities to negotiate in your job—like during promotions, annual reviews, or role changes. These negotiation opportunities usually occur once you are at least a year into your new role but can occur earlier—if you get a promotion, for example.

While you are employed, continue to collect data and do research to ensure that you are being paid fairly. Always take recruiter calls for open jobs, even if you are happily employed. Use these calls to get salary information 1) to see if you are being paid fairly and 2) to use when you try to negotiate internally, during a promotion period or annual review. And continue to check sources like Glassdoor.

Continue to negotiate to ensure that you are fairly compensated now and in the future.

11. SUCCESS IN YOUR NEW JOB

THE SECRET TO MAKING A GREAT FIRST IMPRESSION

Want to know the secret to learning your new job and looking competent while doing it? Ask questions.

This might seem counterintuitive. But often, the most important things to know are precisely those which you could not be expected to know—like team dynamics, company-specific vocabulary, processes, company history, and project details.

You have a limited period of time where you are expected to still be learning—unofficially about six months. Asking tons of questions during this time helps you learn and shows that you can take ownership over your development. Most managers love when their employees take ownership—it's the best thing you can do.

Here are some tips for asking questions during your unofficial six-month learning period:

1. **Make a list of questions.** Carry a notebook with you (a professional-looking one like a Moleskin), and keep a running list of questions. Include things like terms you don't know, project questions, processes you want to learn, or the thing the CEO said in the all-company meeting that you're curious to learn more about.

2. **Ask your manager.** Tell your manager that you are taking the initiative to learn by keeping a list of your questions—and agree on a time to ask her questions on a regular basis. Have a conversation to figure out what works best for you both. Some managers don't mind being interrupted at their desk with questions, while others prefer setting a time to discuss.

3. **Meet the team.** Make a list of people to meet, including team members, managers, and business partners. Schedule meetings with each of these people and brainstorm questions to ask each person in advance. You can ask about their respective roles, their projects, and company initiatives. Use these meeting to learn about each person in addition to the things that will help make you more successful in your new role. See the networking section of this chapter for more.

4. **Ask questions in meetings.** This one can be tricky, so gauge each situation. If you are in an informal meeting with people primarily of your level, feel free to ask questions. But if it's a meeting with senior people, write down your questions to ask your manager later.

5. **Find your "dumb questions" person.** If you can, try to find at the same level who is not on your team and who you get along with well and trust to ask your basic questions.

Another way to learn your job quickly is to ask your manager for learning opportunities, which will contribute to your professional development—and show that you are proactive in taking ownership over your learning. Here are some ways you can ask your manager for learning opportunities:

1. Are there things I can read (e.g., industry newsletters, internal company documents, project history documents)?
2. Are there any meetings I can attend to observe?
3. Are there any projects that someone on the team needs help with?

If your manager says no, continue to ask her every few days—she will likely appreciate the offer.

FEEDBACK, FEEDBACK, FEEDBACK

During a class in business school, my professor and the Chairman of JetBlue, Joel Peterson used to say, "Feedback is the breakfast of champions." Seven years later, I remember his quote and couldn't agree more. Feedback has many benefits, including these three below.

3 KEY BENEFITS OF FEEDBACK

1. **Builds strong relationships.**
   When approached correctly, as outlined below, feedback can strengthen your relationships. Honest dialogue with your manager can help you work more effectively together.

2. **Promotes higher self-awareness.**
   Regular feedback ensures that you are aware of the areas you need to improve—in addition to your key strengths. And regular conversations enable you to discuss your progress with your manager, so that you both recognize it.

3. **Promotes career advancement.**

Regularly and proactively seeking feedback—and acting on it—
shows that you are committed to your self-development and
your career. Having areas for development is not a bad thing.
Everyone has them, including your CEO. Learning what others
view as your key strengths can also help you focus on building
those key points of differentiation. Lastly, having open
discussions around your progress—and your career
aspirations—can be helpful for career advancement.

So, how do you approach these conversations? How do you
ensure that the right feedback structure is in place? And how do you
give your manager feedback if she asks for it? Here are a few tips for
effectively giving and receiving feedback at work:

3 TIPS FOR EFFECTIVE FEEDBACK

1. **Make feedback conversations regular.** Ensure that you have
    regular times to exchange feedback with your manager. If this
    does not exist, work with your manager to create it. You could
    say, "I'm excited about the opportunities here and want to make
    sure that I'm as effective as possible in this role. Regular
    feedback discussions could help. Would you be open to this?"
    Then, figure out what works best for both of you in terms of
    length and frequency. I would recommend aiming for at least
    an hour once a month.

2. **Ask questions.** If you don't understand or disagree with a piece
    of feedback you receive, ask questions. The best feedback
    conversations are a dialogue, and asking questions is the most
    effective way to ensure that you understand the feedback and
    can act on it.

3. **Show how you have improved.** Identify your development
    areas and agree on a plan of action with your manager. For
    example, if you want to improve your presentation skills, agree

on a meeting where you can present slides and practice in advance. Then, after the meeting, review your performance together. The key is to show that you are aware of your development areas and taking proactive steps to address them.

If you are asking for feedback, be prepared to give it. Ask your manager in advance if she wants feedback—and then prepare. The most important thing when delivering feedback is to frame it in a way that others can hear it. Approach feedback discussions with the intent of strengthening relationships, not criticism. Below are specific suggestions for framing feedback.

3 WAYS TO GIVE GREAT FEEDBACK

1. **Be specific—and make it about the behavior.** State the action and the impact. Use this framework: "When you do X, it causes Y." For example, instead of saying, "You need to improve your presentation skills," say, "When you say 'umm' during your presentations, it dilutes the power of your message." The latter is about the behavior, not the person. This is generally much more effective—and better received.

2. **Give strengths first, then areas for development.** Often, people use the feedback sandwich, which goes something like this: "You ask great questions in meetings. But, I wish you would speak up more. But, you are really good at presenting." Good. Bad. Good. Confusing, right? This is the feedback sandwich, and research shows that this confuses the recipient and causes them to focus on the negatives—or not to remember anything at all. A more effective way to give feedback is to discuss strengths first, which makes the person more receptive to the next part of the discussion: areas for development.

3. **Lean positive.** Often, when people give feedback, they breeze through the positive things to get to the areas for development. But research shows that people remember negative things more than positive things. So, when possible, make sure you have more positive things to say than negative, and be specific in your positive examples, describing the positive impact that those strengths have on you and on your relationship.

Prepare your feedback in advance. Spend at least fifteen minutes writing it down, including specific examples. Then, bring your sheet of paper to your meeting to reference. This type of preparation will ensure that you 1) are thoughtful in your feedback and 2) say what you intended.

NETWORKING IN YOUR NEW JOB

You got the job, so you can stop networking, right? Networking is how you get work done in most places, especially if you work cross-functionally. Networking is also how career advancement often happens. Do you know who decides promotions and raises at your new company? Get to know them.

These interactions don't need to feel like networking. Really, it's just getting to know people and learn about things that are happening at your new company And you often end up making friends and finding mentors along the way.

In a prior job, I struck up a conversation in an elevator bank with someone I had never met. Through our two-minute conversation, I learned that he was working on a project that I was interested in. So, I asked if he wanted to grab coffee the next week. He said, "Absolutely—send me an email." So, I did. While I didn't end up working on the project, I did make a new friend at work, who helped me navigate the workplace in my early days. (In many workplaces, "coffee" seems to be the term used for a casual chat, where there often isn't any coffee.)

Approach your networking conversations as casual chats with two objectives: 1) getting to know the person better, and 2) learning more about what's happening at the company. Ask them about their work and lives—their kids, their spouse, their hobbies. Most people like talking about these things, but others are more private and prefer to keep conversation to more work-related topics. Read the situation, and tailor your questions accordingly. Here are some questions you can ask:

- Start with the personal things. How was your weekend? Do you live close to here? Where are you from? Etc.
- How long have you been at the company?
- Can you tell me more about your experience here?
- What other roles have you had?
- What did you do before you joined the company?
- What do you do in your current role?
- What is your favorite project you are working on?
- What else are you working on?

Make it a conversation by asking follow-up questions throughout. Show your interest in the person and their work. Try to learn more about the company, team, ongoing projects and current priorities. These conversations should be casual—do not bring a list of questions. Rather, think of several questions in advance that you want to ask the person—and memorize them. (If you can't remember them, jot them down in your notebook to spark your memory.)

When you start your job, make a list of the people that you want to get to know better. Specifically, include 1) people you will work with (e.g., team, business partners, managers), 2) people who will influence your career progression (e.g., people who decide raises and promotions), and 3) people you like.

Be strategic about what order you chat with people. Start with lower-level people, as you can ask them more basic questions about the company, the work, team dynamics, etc. Once you gain more knowledge, schedule time with the more senior people on your list. Aim to complete these discussions within the first several months of your employment. Then, determine who you want to have regular chats with, and continue to reach out to these people. These include those you work with closely, mentors, friends and those who have a strong impact on your career progression.

Often, people don't prioritize networking with coworkers, even though this is probably the most important thing you can do at work. This is especially true when your work is highly cross-functional.

Often, networking is more important than the work itself.

Networking can also help you get your next role in the company. After starting her new job, Sloane quickly realized that she wanted to work on the sustainability team. She also knew it was difficult to join this team because so many people wanted to do so. A few months into her new job, she reached out to a few members of the sustainability team to have coffee. When they met, she asked if there were any ways she could support the practice.

With the approval of her manager, Sloane ended up organizing monthly sustainability calls and putting together the slide decks for each call. Through these efforts, she built credibility and relationships with the sustainability team. After a year, Sloane was staffed on her first sustainability project—and she now works on that team exclusively.

Networking can also be beneficial if something unexpected happens. Nine months into a prior role, I received some unexpected news: my group was being eliminated. While I was sad to leave this role, I had built relationships with others in the company—and told them about the reorganization. Through these conversations, I found several other great opportunities at the company.

A word about mentorship. People often think that they need to find their next mentor as soon as they join the company. No need to rush—solid relationships take time to build. Instead of aiming to find a mentor through your initial coffee chats, try to identify people you like, admire and trust. Then, continue to ask these people to grab coffee, building these relationships over time.

The best mentor relationships often occur organically over time, usually over at least several months. You don't need to ask, "Will you be my mentor?" And you can have several people you consider to be mentors. At my last company, I had at least five people I went to for career advice and who I later learned were great advocates behind the scenes, and I am grateful to each of them.

Forming close relationships with coworkers will enhance your ability to get things done, contribute to your career advancement, and make work so much more fun. So, get some coffees on your calendar, go to the company happy hours, and chat with people you don't know in the kitchen, elevator banks and hallways.

PLAN FOR YOUR NEXT PROMOTION

You may be wondering why we are already talking about promotion. You just got the job. But career advancement often requires early planning.

Marissa Mayer, the recent CEO of Yahoo, stated this well. When discussing her impressive career trajectory at Google, she said, "I got every single one of [my promotions] by asking and getting feedback and planning for it." She asked targeted questions, like "If I want to be a director of product management, what would that look like? What would it take?"

Job performance is important for promotion. But,

> **To be promoted, it's not enough simply to be good at your job.**

You must understand how career advancement works, be

strategic in your approach, and advocate for yourself. You also must figure out when it makes sense to have the discussions.

Often, the best thing to do when you start is to figure out how career advancement works at your company—with no discussion around promotion. Wait until you feel that it's appropriate to initiate the discussions around moving to the next level. This will likely be a minimum of six months, and often more like a year.

Also, you may not want to be promoted soon, and that's entirely okay. Being promoted can entail more work—and often more stress. Understandably, many people don't want to take on expanded career responsibilities at certain points in their lives. Here are some reasons I've heard: "I'm a new dad and don't want to work the extra hours." "I don't want to manage a larger team—it's too stressful." "I want more time to pursue interests outside of work." Think back to your priorities and values, and pursue promotions accordingly.

5 CRITICAL STEPS FOR PROMOTION

1. Understand how career advancement works.

Many companies don't have standard criteria for promotion. How can you move to the next level if you don't know how performance management works? Ask.

And, ask early—like Marissa Mayer did. You can frame the discussion with your manager in a growth-oriented way by saying, "I'm excited about the opportunities at this company. I'm curious to learn more about how performance management works as I think about developing my career here." Then, ask the following questions:

- How does performance management work? (i.e. Are there criteria that determine promotion?)
- Who assesses my performance? (Just my manager? The whole team?)

- When do performance reviews occur? (Annually? Semiannually?)
- What would it take to move to the next level? (Specifically, what would I need to do? Is promotion possible in my current role?)

Taking the initiative to have this conversation shows your commitment to personal development—and your desire to contribute to the company over the long term.

Having this conversation early will give you tangible goals to work towards, and it will help you understand the opportunities that could exist in the future. Sometimes, promotion can only occur if there's a vacant role. Knowing these things upfront can be helpful as you start to plan your career.

2. Express your interest in moving to the next level.

Sitting back and hoping someone notices all the great work you do is unlikely to lead to a promotion.

Usually, you must express your interest. You can say something like, "I'm excited about the career opportunities here and would like to further contribute to the team. What would it take to make it to the next level?"

Consider when it makes sense to ask this question—I recommend a minimum of six months. Try to figure out what's typical in terms of length of time it takes to make it to the next level, and know that it could take several months, or years, for a promotion to happen.

Asking the question won't guarantee that it happens quickly—but it starts the dialogue. If your manager seems receptive and you want to be promoted, continue to discuss it in your regular feedback discussions—more below.

If you have been there for several years, take the same approach of asking a question: *What would it take to get to the next level?* What doesn't work well is saying things like "I've been here for three years and want to be promoted." Instead, frame it in terms of what you can offer and ask the question of what it would take to make it to the next level.

3. Have regular performance discussions with your manager.

Once you've expressed your desire to move to the next level, continue to discuss it with your manager in your regular performance management discussions. You can ask these questions each time:

- Do you have any feedback for me? (Be prepared to provide feedback to your manager as well.)
- Am I on track to move to the next level? (Only ask this once you've expressed a desire to move to the next level.)
- What do I need to ensure that I stay on track?

Make it a discussion. Ask questions—and really try to understand what it takes and where you stand. Also, make sure that you are explicitly showing your manager all the great work you are doing. In his book *Power*, Jeffrey Pfeffer, a professor at Stanford Business School, says,

> *Your first responsibility is to ensure that those at higher levels in your company know what you are accomplishing. And the best way to ensure they know what you are achieving is to tell them.*

Explicitly show your manager your contributions by doing the following:

- **Write down your accomplishments—and review them regularly.** For each monthly development conversation, prepare a document listing your goals and accomplishments for that time period. Review it together to ensure that your manager is aware of what you have done.

- **Send weekly update emails.** Another way to keep your manager apprised of your work is by 1) sending her an email each Monday with your top priorities and goals for the week, and 2) sending her an email on Friday highlighting what you have accomplished that week. If you take this approach, first have a verbal conversation with your manager to establish this process. And make sure your emails are bullet-pointed and easy to read quickly.

4. Act like you're already at the next level.

The best way to earn a promotion is to excel in your job—and act like you are already at the next level. This shows that you are already ready for the next level, which makes it easier for people to think about promoting you. Here are a couple of powerful ways to display your readiness:

- **Ask for "stretch" projects.** Ask your manager if there are any special projects you can do to prepare you for the next level.

- **Own your work.** As a manager, one of the top things I look for in promoting members of my team is the ability of employees to "own" their work. Can they problem-solve on their own? Can they influence others? Can they complete entire work streams without constant guidance? This requires figuring out when and how to engage your manager—and some of this is dependent on their own style. (No need to focus on this one until you have ramped up in your new role, which usually takes at least six months.)

5. Get to know the decision-makers.

Figure out who is involved in your promotion decision. If the decision requires approval from more than just your manager, then it's time to network and make some connections. Ask to grab coffee with them. Get to know them.

People promote people that they like, so start forming strong connections early with the people who hold the power to promote you. If you can, try to work with them on a project so you can demonstrate your talents.

What do you do once you get promoted? There are two things to consider: 1) negotiation and 2) setting yourself up for success in your new role. Being promoted is the optimal time to try to negotiate again.

Even more importantly, ask yourself: *What you need to succeed in your new role?* Additional team members? A larger budget? Support from certain leaders? Then, ask for these things and make a clear case for why you need them. Try to create a structure that will enable you to succeed in your new role.

YOUR NEXT JOB

When you're ready to move to a new job, remember what you learned in this book. Perhaps even pick it up again. The skills you developed will enable you to find positions you love throughout your long career, which will lead to more happiness at work—and in life. And that's something worth pursuing.

Above all, remember: A job is only great when it's a match on *both* sides.

APPENDIX

A. COMMON INTERVIEW QUESTIONS

Walk me through your resume.

What are your strengths?

What are your weaknesses?

Why are you interested in working at this company?

Why do you want this job?

Where do you see yourself in five years? Ten years?

Why do you want to leave your current company?

Why was there a gap in your employment between [insert date] and [insert date]?

What can you offer us that someone else cannot?

What are three things your former manager would like you to improve on?

Are you willing to relocate?

Are you willing to travel?

Tell me about an accomplishment you are most proud of.

Tell me about a time you made a mistake.

What is your dream job?

How did you hear about this position?

What would you like to accomplish in the first 30 days/60 days/90 days on the job?

Discuss your educational background.

Tell me how you handled a difficult situation.

Why should we hire you?

Why are you looking for a new job?

Tell me about a time you dealt with a difficult situation at work.

How would you deal with an angry customer?

What are your salary requirements?

Describe a time when you went above and beyond the requirements for a project.

Who are our competitors?

What was your biggest failure?

What motivates you?

What's your availability?

Tell me about a time when you disagreed with your boss.

How do you handle pressure?

What are your career goals?

What would your direct reports say about you?

If I called your manager right now and asked her to name an area that you could improve on, what would she say?

Are you a leader or a follower?

What was the last book you read for fun?

What are your hobbies?

What makes you uncomfortable?

What are some of your leadership experiences?

How would you fire someone?

What do you like the most and least about working in this industry?

What questions haven't I asked you?

What questions do you have for me?

B. INTERVIEW STRUCTURE BY ROUND

Recruiter Screen
Format: Phone
Who: Recruiter
Length: 30 minutes
Key Questions:

- Talk me through your resume/background.
- Why do you want this role?
- Why do you want to work at this company?
- What are your compensation expectations?
- Do you have any questions for me?

First-Round Interview
Format: Phone (sometimes video or in-person)
Who: Hiring Manager (i.e., your future manager)—can involve others as well
Length: 30 minutes
Key Questions:

- Same as recruiter questions
- Do you have any questions for me? (Make sure you do.)

Second-Round Interview:
Format: In-person (sometimes video)
Who: Hiring Manager + Other Employees (2-8)
Length: 30 minutes to 1 hour with each person
Key Questions:

- See Chapter 7
- See Appendix

NOTES

INTRODUCTION

Research indicates that being happy in your work also leads to greater career success: Bonnie Marcus, "Happiness at Work: The Relationship Between Happiness and Career Advancement," *Forbes*, November 18, 2011, accessed January 13, 2018, https://www.forbes.com/sites/bonniemarcus/2011/11/18/happiness-at-work-the-relationship-between-happiness-and-career-advancement/#5b6d1eb87c61.

The average person spends 60 percent of their waking weekday hours at work: Lydia Saad, "The '40-Hour' Workweek Is Actually Longer——by Seven Hours," *Gallup News*, August 29, 2014, accessed May 26, 2017, http://news.gallup.com/poll/175286/hour-workweek-actually-longer-seven-hours.aspx.

Most people have fourteen to twenty different jobs over the course of their careers: This assumes a sixty-year career. Jeanne Meister, "The Future of Work: Job Hopping Is the 'New Normal' for Millennials," *Forbes*, August 14, 2012, accessed May 26, 2017, https://www.forbes.com/sites/jeannemeister/2012/08/14/the-future-of-work-job-hopping-is-the-new-normal-for-millennials/#783e209313b8.

85 percent of jobs are obtained through networking, *not* through online resume drops: Lou Adler, "New Survey Reveals 85% of All Jobs are Filled Via Networking," LinkedIn, February 29, 2016, accessed June 2, 2017, https://www.linkedin.com/pulse/new-survey-reveals-85-all-jobs-filled-via-networking-lou-adler.

50 percent of open jobs are *not* posted online: Kathryn Dill, "Study: Half of All Available Jobs Are Never Advertised," *Forbes*, August 20, 2014, accessed June 2, 2017, https://www.forbes.com/sites/kathryndill/2014/08/20/study-half-of-all-available-jobs-are-never-advertised-publicly/#22c62bd324fe.

Most people . . . miss out on $500k+ over their lifetime: "Most People Don't Negotiate Due to Fear & Lack of Skills," Salary.com, 2016, accessed May 26, 2017, https://www.salary.com/most-people-don-t-negotiate-due-to-fear-lack-of-skills/.

millennials are projected to change jobs even more often: Jeanne Meister, "The Future of Work: Job Hopping Is the 'New Normal' for Millennials," *Forbes*, August 14, 2012, accessed May 26, 2017, https://www.forbes.com/sites/jeannemeister/2012/08/14/the-future-of-work-job-hopping-is-the-new-normal-for-millennials/#783e209313b8.

CHAPTER 1

80 percent of Americans are unhappy at work, yet only 20 percent planning to look for a new job: Andrew Soergel, "2016 Could Be the Year of the Job-Hopper," *U.S. News & World Report*, December 28, 2015, accessed January 13, 2018, https://www.usnews.com/news/articles/2015-12-28/2016-could-be-the-year-of-the-job-hopper; Alyson Shontell, "80% Hate Their Jobs——But Should You Choose a Passion or a Paycheck?," *Business Insider*, October 4, 2010, accessed January 13, 2018, http://www.businessinsider.com/what-do-you-do-when-you-hate-your-job-2010-10.

"getting fired from Apple was the best thing": Steve Jobs, commencement address, Stanford University, June 12, 2005, prepared text, accessed January 13, 2018, https://news.stanford.edu/2005/06/14/jobs-061505/.

"people who are happy in their jobs": Bonnie Marcus, "Happiness At Work: The Relationship Between Happiness and Career Advancement," *Forbes*, November 18, 2011, accessed January 13, 2018, https://www.forbes.com/sites/bonniemarcus/2011/11/18/happiness-at-work-the-relationship-between-happiness-and-career-advancement/#5b6d1eb87c61.

CHAPTER 2

cultural fit leads to greater job satisfaction, longer tenure, and superior job performance: Katie Bouton, "Recruiting for Cultural Fit," *Harvard Business Review*, July 17, 2015, accessed January 13, 2018, https://hbr.org/2015/07/recruiting-for-cultural-fit; Amy L. Kristof-Brown, Ryan D. Zimmerman, and Erin C. Johnson, "Consequences of Individuals' Fit at Work: A Meta-Analysis of Person–Job, Person–Organization, Person–Group, and Person–Supervisor Fit," *Personnel Psychology* 58, no. 2 (Summer 2005): 281-342, accessed January 13, 2018, http://nreilly.asp.radford.edu/kristof-brown%20et%20al.pdf.

"close work friendships boost work satisfaction by 50 percent": Christine M. Riordan, "We All Need Friends at Work," *Harvard Business Review*, July 3, 2013, accessed January 13, 2018, https://hbr.org/2013/07/we-all-need-friends-at-work.

"remember negative things more strongly and in more detail": Hara Estroff Marano, "Our Brain's Negative Bias: Why Our Brains Are More Highly Attuned to Negative News," *Psychology*

Today, June 20, 2003, last reviewed June 9, 2016, accessed January 13, 2018, https://www.psychologytoday.com/articles/200306/our-brains-negative-bias.

exceptional leaders are "really outstanding at doing a few things well": John H. Zenger, Joseph R. Folkman, Robert H. Sherwin, Jr., and Barbara A. Steel, *How to Be Exceptional: Drive Leadership Success by Magnifying Your Strengths* (New York: McGraw-Hill, 2012), XIII.

work/life balance is a strong predictor of happiness: Jayson DeMers, "How to Be Happier at Work, According to Scientific Studies," NBC News, March 24, 2017, accessed January 13, 2018, https://www.nbcnews.com/better/careers/how-be-happier-work-it-s-easier-you-think-n738081.

above $75,000, money does not lead to greater happiness: Mark Fahey, "Money Can Buy Happiness, but Only to a Point," CNBC, December 14, 2015, accessed January 13, 2018, http://www.cnbc.com/2015/12/14/money-can-buy-happiness-but-only-to-a-point.html.

CHAPTER 3

Michael Jordan: "Michael Jordan Didn't Make Varsity–At First," *Newsweek*, October 17, 2015, accessed May 26, 2017, http://www.newsweek.com/missing-cut-382954.

"I've missed more than 9,000 shots . . . why I succeed": Michael Jordan, quoted in "Celebs Who Went from Failures to Success Stories," CBS News, accessed May 26, 2017, http://www.cbsnews.com/pictures/celebs-who-went-from-failures-to-success-stories/8/.

Oprah Winfrey: "Celebs Who Went from Failures to Success Stories," CBS News, accessed May 26, 2017, http://www.cbsnews.com/pictures/celebs-who-went-from-failures-to-success-stories/10/.

Steven Spielberg: "Celebs Who Went from Failures to Success Stories," CBS News, accessed May 26, 2017, http://www.cbsnews.com/pictures/celebs-who-went-from-failures-to-success-stories/9/.

Lady Gaga: "Lady Gaga," *Wikipedia*, accessed May 26, 2017, https://en.wikipedia.org/wiki/Lady_Gaga.

Sidney Poitier: "Celebs Who Went from Failures to Success Stories," CBS News, accessed May 26, 2017, https://www.cbsnews.com/pictures/celebs-who-went-from-failures-to-success-stories/7/.

Bill Gates: "Traf-O-Data," *Wikipedia*, accessed May 26, 2017, https://en.wikipedia.org/wiki/Traf-O-Data; "Celebs Who Went from Failures to Success Stories," CBS News, accessed May 26, 2017, https://www.cbsnews.com/pictures/celebs-who-went-from-failures-to-success-stories/.

Vera Wang: "Vera Wang," *Wikipedia*, accessed May 26, 2017, https://en.wikipedia.org/wiki/Vera_Wang.

Thomas Edison: "Thomas Edison," *Wikipedia*, accessed May 26, 2017, https://en.wikipedia.org/wiki/Thomas_Edison; "Celebs Who Went from Failures to Success Stories," CBS News, accessed May 26, 2017, http://www.cbsnews.com/pictures/celebs-who-went-from-failures-to-success-stories/6/.

Growth Mindset/Fixed Mindset: Carol S. Dweck, *Mindset: The New Psychology of Success*, 2nd ed. (New York: Random House, 2016), 23, Kindle.

"Think of times other people outdid you . . . You can do that, too, if you want to": Carol S. Dweck, *Mindset: The New Psychology of Success*, 2nd ed. (New York: Random House, 2016), 1732, Kindle.

"same areas of the brain become activated when we experience rejection as when we experience physical pain": Kirsten Weir, "The Pain of Social Rejection," *Monitor on Psychology* 43, no. 4 (April 2012), accessed May 26, 2017, http://www.apa.org/monitor/2012/04/rejection.aspx.

"A remarkable thing I've learned . . . plunge into it wholeheartedly and stick to it": Carol S. Dweck, *Mindset: The New Psychology of Success*, 2nd ed. (New York: Random House, 2016), 959, Kindle.

CHAPTER 4

On average, recruiters spend six seconds "reading" each resume: "Keeping an Eye on Recruiter Behavior: New Study Clarifies Recruiter Decision-Making," Ladders, 2012, accessed January 20, 2018, https://cdn.theladders.net/static/images/basicSite/pdfs/TheLadders-EyeTracking-StudyC2.pdf.

Men apply for a job when they meet only 60 percent of the qualifications, but women often apply only if they meet 100 percent: Tara Sophia Mohr, "Why Women Don't Apply for Jobs Unless They're 100% Qualified," *Harvard Business Review*, August 25, 2014, accessed January 20, 2018, https://hbr.org/2014/08/why-women-dont-apply-for-jobs-unless-theyre-100-qualified.

CHAPTER 5

85 percent of jobs are acquired through networking: Lou Adler, "New Survey Reveals 85% of All Jobs are Filled Via Networking," LinkedIn, February 29, 2016, accessed June 2, 2017, https://www.linkedin.com/pulse/new-survey-reveals-85-all-jobs-filled-via-networking-lou-adler.

people drastically underestimated the number of people who would help them—by up to 50 percent: Marguerite Rigoglioso, "Francis Flynn: If You Want Something, Ask for It," *Stanford Business*, July 1, 2008, accessed January 14, 2018, https://www.gsb.stanford.edu/insights/francis-flynn-if-you-want-something-ask-it.

"Connection is why we're here. It's what gives purpose and meaning to our lives": Brené Brown, "The Power of Vulnerability" (video of TED talk, TEDxHouston, June 2010), accessed January 14, 2018, https://www.ted.com/talks/brene_brown_on_vulnerability.

CHAPTER 7

"Connection Effect": Tanya Menon and Leigh Thompson, "Why You Should Always Go Off-Script in a Job Interview," *Harvard Business Review*, July 14, 2016, accessed January 15, 2018, https://hbr.org/2016/07/why-you-should-always-go-off-script-in-a-job-interview.

interviewers make a hiring decision in the first seven minutes:
Ellie Zolfagharifard, "First Impressions Really Do Count:
Employers Make Decisions about Job Applicants in Under Seven
Minutes," *Daily Mail*, June 18, 2014, updated June 19, 2014,
accessed January 15, 2018,
http://www.dailymail.co.uk/sciencetech/article-2661474/First-
impressions-really-DO-count-Employers-make-decisions-job-
applicants-seven-minutes.html.

CHAPTER 8

**"We want people who are problem solvers . . . who act like
they own the place":** Ken
Blanchard, Susan Fowler, and Laurence Hawkins, *Self Leadership and
the One Minute Manager: Increasing Effectiveness through Situational Self
Leadership* (New York: William Morrow, 2005).

the first fifteen seconds of an interview: Rosie Ifould, "Acting
on impulse," *The Guardian*, March
6, 2009, accessed January 15, 2018,
https://www.theguardian.com/lifeandstyle/2009/mar/07/first-
impressions-snap-decisions-impulse.

People hire people that they like: Drake Baer, "If You Want to
Get Hired, Act Like Your Potential
Boss," *Business Insider*, May 29, 2014, accessed January 15, 2018,
http://www.businessinsider.com/managers-hire-people-who-
remind-them-of-themselves-2014-5.

CHAPTER 10

**People who don't negotiate miss out on $500k—or more—
over their lifetime:** "Most People Don't Negotiate Due to Fear &

Lack of Skills," Salary.com, 2016, accessed May 26, 2017,
https://www.salary.com/most-people-don-t-negotiate-due-to-fear-
lack-of-skills/.

two million meals to people who are hungry in the Bay Area:
SF-Marin Food Bank, accessed January 17, 2018,
https://www.sfmfoodbank.org/about/.

**only 37 percent of people say that they consistently
negotiate salary:** "Most People Don't Negotiate Due to Fear &
Lack of Skills," Salary.com, 2016, accessed May 26, 2017,
https://www.salary.com/most-people-don-t-negotiate-due-to-fear-
lack-of-skills/.

**Women are four times less likely to negotiate than men . . .
and receive 30 percent less than men:** Linda Babcock and Sara
Laschever, *Women Don't Ask: Negotiation and the Gender Divide*, 1st
ed. (Princeton, NJ: Princeton University Press, 2003).

a life-changing negotiation book: Linda Babcock and Sara
Laschever, *Women Don't Ask: Negotiation and the Gender Divide*, 1st
ed. (Princeton, NJ: Princeton University Press, 2003).

**"when people cease to see negotiation as a fight . . .
opportunities to negotiate":** Paraphrase of Margaret Neale and
Thomas Lys, authors of *Getting (More of) What You Want*, by
Elizabeth MacBride, "Margaret Neale: Five Steps to Better
Negotiating," *Stanford Business*, July 16, 2015, accessed May 26,
2017, https://www.gsb.stanford.edu/insights/margaret-neale-five-
steps-better-negotiating.

CHAPTER 11

"Feedback is the breakfast of champions": Joel Peterson, "Feedback is the Breakfast of Champions: 10 Tips for Doing it Right," LinkedIn, October 11, 2013, accessed January 17, 2018, https://www.linkedin.com/pulse/20131011052926-11846967-feedback-is-the-breakfast-of-champions-10-tips-for-doing-it-right.

the feedback sandwich: Adam Grant, "Stop Serving the Feedback Sandwich," LinkedIn, May 3, 2016, accessed January 17, 2018, https://www.linkedin.com/pulse/stop-serving-feedback-sandwich-adam-grant.

"Lean positive": Joel Peterson, "Feedback is the Breakfast of Champions: 10 Tips for Doing it Right," LinkedIn, October 11, 2013, accessed January 17, 2018, https://www.linkedin.com/pulse/20131011052926-11846967-feedback-is-the-breakfast-of-champions-10-tips-for-doing-it-right.

people remember negative things more than positive things: Alina Tugend, "Praise Is Fleeting, but Brickbats We Recall," *New York Times*, March 23, 2012, accessed January 17, 2018, http://www.nytimes.com/2012/03/24/your-money/why-people-remember-negative-events-more-than-positive-ones.html.

"I got every single one of [my promotions] by asking and getting feedback and planning for it"; "If I want to be a director of product management . . . What would it take?": Marissa Mayer, quoted in Bill Snyder, "Marissa Mayer: Do Something You Feel Unprepared To Do," *Stanford Business*, April 12, 2017, accessed January 17, 2018.

"Your first responsibility . . . tell them": Jeffrey Pfeffer, *Power* (HarperCollins e-books, 2010), Kindle.

People promote people that they like: Sue Shellenbarger, "Why Likability Matters More at Work," *Wall Street Journal*, March 25,

2014, accessed January 17, 2018,
https://www.wsj.com/articles/why-likability-matters-more-at-work-1395788402.

APPENDIX A: COMMON INTERVIEW QUESTIONS

Jacquelyn Smith, "How to Ace the 50 Most Common Interview Questions," *Forbes*, January 11, 2013, accessed January 20, 2018, https://www.forbes.com/sites/jacquelynsmith/2013/01/11/how-to-ace-the-50-most-common-interview-questions/#3008b0b4624d.

ACKNOWLEDGMENTS

Thank you to my husband, Robin, who read draft after draft over the past two years and provided invaluable support and encouragement. I am grateful that we are on this life journey together. And thank you to my amazing son, Ever—who has provided infinite inspiration since his arrival into the world last year.

A huge thank you to two very special Elizabeths. Elizabeth Pederson, thank you for inviting me to take my first writing class—and for all your support, encouragement, information and help. You are an incredible writer and a savvy editor—your input over the past two years has made this book what it is today.

Elizabeth Geri, thank you for being such a wonderful manager, mentor and friend. And thank you for your review of the entire book—your suggestions, as always, made it so much better. (Thank you as well to all the other amazing work mentors throughout my career—you know who you are, I hope.)

Thank you to Liz Downey, an immensely talented graphic designer, who developed the cover for this book and shared her ideas on how to get it out into the world. Her beautiful, and inspiring, products can be found at <u>Two Tumbleweeds</u>.

I also want to thank all the people who helped make this book happen by sharing great insights and ideas, specifically Francesca Baraggioli Sanday, Meghan Bot-Miller, Micah Bot-Miller, Chrissy Braden, Delano Brissett, Shuvo Chatterjee, Stephanie Cho, Amy Cole, Bijel Doshi, Brahim Elbouchikhi, Patrick Fitzgerald, Danielle Garcia, Sarah Groen, Dusty Gronso, Kate Gronso, Aliisa Hodges, Mili Khandheria, Jing Lee, Aabed Meer, Christina Millikin, Tim Millikin, Lisa Newman-Wise, Yoshio Osaki, Aden Pavkov, Pam Pavkov, Jackie Peterson, Li Qiu, Katie Reyero, Lexi Sack, JP Sanday, Alex Tonelli, Charlotte Will, Tyler Will, Dana Worth and those who provided ideas anonymously as well. I am so grateful to you all.

A few more people deserve a very special note. Thank you to Angela Rastegar, who read an entire early draft of the book and provided valuable feedback and encouraged me to start publishing my writing on Medium. Thank you to Alexandra Golden for the ideas, inspiration and edits—I'm so grateful to you for lending your talents to this project. Thank you to Liz Downey, Lindsay Ferstandig, Chris Robb and Grace Yokoi for the ideas on how to get this book out into the world.

Thank you to my editor, Michelle Turner, who ensured that this book was grammatically correct and formatted all the footnotes. She can be found at thewordforward.com.

Last but certainly not least, I want to thank my mom and dad for giving me the foundation to write this book—and for the love and support, as well as my sister and the entire Bot-Miller family.

And to all those who provided kind words, which sparked me to continue, even on the most challenging days.

ABOUT THE AUTHOR

 Heather Hund has worked at companies including Goldman Sachs, Boston Consulting Group and Gap Inc. and has over a decade of experience in strategy, management, operations, investing, marketing, branding—and building and hiring teams. She holds an MBA from Stanford and an MA in Art History from Oxford.

Personally, Heather enjoys creating art, reading non-fiction, running, skiing, and desert road trips. She lives in San Francisco with her husband, son—and Golden Retriever, Ollie.

Heather can be found at www.artofthejobsearch.co, at @heatherhund on Medium, and @heather_hund on Twitter.